Hebrew with Joy!

Learn Simple Hebrew with the Scriptures

Joy Carroll

Hebrew with Joy!

©2019 by SimkhaPress
ISBN: 978-1-7333230-1-7

Unless otherwise noted, Scriptures are from The Holy Bible, Tree of Life Version (TLV) © 2011, 2012, 2013, 2014 & 2015 by the Messianic Jewish Family Bible Society.

Scripture quotations marked NIV are taken from The Holy Bible, New International Version® NIV® Copyright © 1973, 1978, 1984, 2011 by Biblica, Inc.™ Used by permission.

All rights reserved. No part of this publication may be reproduced, stored or transmitted in any form or by any means, including photocopying, recording, or other technology, without the written permission of the publisher.

Paleo-Hebrew for "shalom" used with permission by Dr. I Suuquina
http://www.indigenousmessengers.com

The websites cited in this book were active at time of publishing. There is no guarantee that they will continue to be available in the future.

For supplemental products for use with this book, visit: http://HebrewWithJoy.com

Rev. Date: 3-25-21

הֹדוּ לַיהוָה כִּי־טוֹב כִּי לְעוֹלָם חַסְדּוֹ:

Psalm 107:1 *Praise ADONAI, for He is good,
for His lovingkindness endures forever.*

Hebrew with Joy! (HWJ) is dedicated to my husband, Russ,
who has always encouraged me to follow my dreams!

Todah Rabah (thanks very much) to:
HWJ Prayer Team: your faithfulness to pray for me through
this project provided the encouragement, inspiration,
strength and energy to complete HWJ
Graphic Designer: our wonderful daughter, Becca Kendall
HWJ Editing Team:
Pam Neilson, Jackie Newman, Erin Miskey, Natasha Cinkosky,
Juliet Rizzo, Gaylyn Williams, Adam Haeffner, Cecilia Mikolajczak,
Alleluyah Williams, Marion Torrez
Proofing: Linda Harris
Website Support: Joshua Morgan, Pat Cohen, Deb Wiley
Author Photo: Randie Ide
Publishing Support: Gordon Saunders, Greg Wiley
Audio Editor: Daveed Vogt
Software Support: Jeremy Begley
Inspiration Launch Team: Margie Wood, Esh Gray
Marketing: Olenka Nakka

A very special thanks to our congregations, Etz Khayim and Kol Dodi,
for supporting and encouraging my Hebrew classes over the years.

Todah rabah (thanks so much) to all of my Hebrew students, who,
for the past six years, have contributed ideas and suggestions
to make this book more complete and user-friendly!

Table of Contents

Introduction 7
Course Syllabus 9
Alef Bet Song 13
Lesson 1 ב שׁ ת 15
Lesson 2 ל מ ם 21
Lesson 3 ר י ה 27
Lesson 4 נ ן ע א 33
Lesson 5 כ ך ח 39
Lesson 6 ד ב ו 49
Lesson 7 פּ ז צ ץ 55
Lesson 8 פ ף ק כ 61
Lesson 9 שׂ ס ט ג 69
Lesson 10   Reading Scriptures 79
Lesson Fill-Ins 94
Hebrew Letters 96
Hebrew Vowels 98
Hebrew Phrases 100
Hebrew Resources 101
Scriptural and Cultural Treasures Index 103
Hebrew Dictionary 105

Introduction

Shalom and welcome to **Hebrew with Joy!**
Yes, you really can learn to read and write Hebrew, the Holy Language of the Living God! Learning to read the original Hebrew of the Bible will bring you a greater understanding of the heart of Adonai (God.)

Video Lesson Files are now included in your book purchase for no extra charge! When used together with the book, you will have a complete learning experience, almost like a live class! The videos can be downloaded at:
hebrewwithjoy.com/hebrew-with-joy-video-lessons-2/   password: HWJvideos

Audio files which record the Hebrew for each lesson are also available for no charge. The files can be accessed on our website: https://hebrewwithjoy.com/audio-files/

Pronunciation: Hebrew with Joy! teaches the *Sephardic* form of pronunciation to honor the standard pronunciation used in Israel.

English Transliterations and Accented Syllables in this book are based on the following chart:

English Transliteration Sounds			
a	"a" as in all	kh	"ch" as in Bach
e	"e" as in egg	ay	"ay" as is lay
ee	"ee" as in feet	ai	"i" as in pie
o	"o" as in over	oy	"oy" as in boy
oo	"oo" as in too	ooey	"ooey" as in gooey
CAPITAL letters show the accented syllable in a word as in "sha-LOM"			
If the accent is *not* on the last syllable, it will be **BOLD** as in "**E**-rev"			

Suggestions for Students:

- Try to study with a partner. The accountability and interaction will aid in learning.
- Create your own flashcards as each new letter, vowel, root and key word is introduced. Then practice every day!
- Try *not* to write the Hebrew transliterations (English sounds) above the Hebrew in the book! This will slow down the learning process.
- If this is your first Hebrew class, practice writing in block letters. If you know the Alef-Bet already, take the challenge to learn script, which is the standard of writing in Israel. (Refer to the Hebrew Letter pages in the Appendix)
- After each lesson is taught, use the learning activity that goes with the lesson. It will reinforce the materials in a fun, up-beat way.
- Listen to the audio files between class sessions to reinforce the new letter and vowel sounds as you practice your pronunciation.
- Have fun as you learn the language of God!

Suggestions for Teachers:

- ***Hebrew with Joy! Teacher's Guide*** is now available! The guide is full of helpful teaching suggestions and includes all fill-in answers, supply list, graduation certificates and much more. It can be ordered through Amazon or at: https://hebrewwithjoy.com/teachers/

- Answers to Lesson Exercises can be found on this web page: HebrewWithJoy.com/HWJ-exercise-answers   Password: answers

- Encourage students to listen to the **audio files** between class sessions. This will especially help the audio learners. They can be downloaded at: https://hebrewwithjoy.com/audio-files/   Password: listen

- **Video Lesson Files** are an excellent teaching tool. The files are available for downloading at: https://hebrewwithjoy.com/hebrew-with-joy-video-lessons-2/

Course Syllabus

New Key Word		New Root		New Vowels	New Letters	#
Sabbath	שַׁבָּת	rest, stop	שׁ.ב.ת	ַ ּ	שׁ ב ת	1
peace	שָׁלוֹם	completion wholeness	שׁ.ל.ם	וֹ	ל מ ם	2
instruction	תּוֹרָה	hit the mark	י.ר.ה	ָ ֳ ֹ	ה ר י	3
hear/listen	שְׁמַע	hear and obey	שׁ.מ.ע	ׁ ְ ֱ	נ ן ע א	4
blessed	בָּרוּךְ	bless, kneel	ב.ר.ך	וּ ֲ	כ ד ך ח	5
love	אַהֲבָה	love	א.ה.ב	ח ֲ	ד ב ו	6
life	חַיִּים	live	ח.י.ה	ִי ֵ	צ ץ פ ז	7
holy	קָדוֹשׁ	holy	ק.ד.שׁ	ָ	פ ף כ ק	8
joy	שִׂמְחָה	joyful	שׂ.מ.ח	וִ וְ	ט ג שׂ ס	9
Reading Scriptures						10

Hebrew with Joy!   Course Syllabus

**Please complete this page without looking up any answers.
This evaluates your Hebrew knowledge before the class.

Name: _____

Date: _____   # Pre-Quiz

A. Is this your first Hebrew class? _____

B. Match the letters to their sounds:

ע 3   1. d

צ ___   2. r

פ ___   3. silent

ר ___   4. s

ק ___   5. k

ד ___   6. ts

ס ___   7. p

C. Match the sounds:

תְּ ___   1. too

תוֹ ___   2. tee

תַ ___   3. tai (tie)

תוּ ___   4. tah

תִי ___   5. toe

תֵי ___   6. teh

תֶ ___   7. tay

D. Match the words:

שְׁמַע ___   1. life

קָדוֹשׁ ___   2. blessed

חַיִּים ___   3. holy

בָּרוּךְ ___   4. hear

E. Match the roots:

שׂ.מ.ח ___   1. instruction

י.ר.ה ___   2. love

שׁ.ב.ת ___   3. joy

א.ה.ב ___   4. rest/stop

E. Write in Hebrew: Sabbath Peace   _____

Alef Bet Song

By Debbie Friedman
Search Online: Debbie Friedman Alef Bet Video
Please note: some letter names have been changed to match the letter sounds

ב ב א
Vet Bet **A**-lef

ה ד ג
Hay **DA**-let **GI**-mel

ט ח ז ו
Tet Khet **ZA**-yin Vav

כ כ י
Kaf Khaf Yud

נ מ ל
Nun Mem **LA**-med

פ ע ס
Fay Pay **A**-yin **SA**-mekh

ר ק צ
Raysh Koof **TSA**-dee

ת ש שׁ
Tav Sin Shin

Hebrew with Joy!   Lesson 1   ב ת שׁ

Lesson 1   בּ ת שׁ

Israeli Greeting
Hello! My name is _____.   shalom! sh-mee _____.

A - Letters

Sound	Name	Letter	
"**b**" as in **b**ar (Bet has a **b**ottom **b**ar)	Bet (with a middle dot)	בּ	A1
"**t**" as in **t**oe (Tav has a toe)	Tav	ת	A2
"**sh**" as in **sh**ine	Shin (dot on top right)	שׁ	A3

> The very first Hebrew word in Scripture is "b-re-SHEET" בְּרֵאשִׁית. *(Genesis 1:1)*
> It means "in the beginning" and includes the three new letters. "b-re-SHEET" comes from the Hebrew root meaning "head, beginning, first or front" and is also the root of the Hebrew word "rosh" (head). Just as the LORD created the heavens and the earth, He also promises that He "will make you the head [rosh] and not the tail." (Deuteronomy 28:13 NIV, emphasis added).   A4

Read Hebrew from right to left!   A5

Read the names of the letters on the next line, then, read the sounds of the letters:

ת בּ שׁ בּ שׁ ת שׁ בּ ת בּ שׁ ⇐   A6

B - Vowels

Sound	Vowel	
"a" as in all	◌ַ	B2
"a" as in all	◌ָ	B3

◌ = *any letter*   B1

Say the letter sound first, then the vowel (hint: think "up, down"): בַּ = "b" + "a" = "ba"   B4

שָׁ תָ בַּ שַׁ בָּ שָׁ בַּ תָ תַּ בָּ   B5

(hint: think "up, down, left"): תָּשׁ "t" + "a" + "sh" = "tash"   B6

_____ בַּת תַת שַׁב בַּב שָׁת תַשׁ בָּשׁ   B7

For English meaning see Lesson Fill-Ins

Lesson 1 ב ת ש *Hebrew with Joy!*

B8 *In Hebrew Sephardic pronunciation, <u>most</u> words are accented on the **last** syllable.
 * Example with two letters and two vowels: בַּתָ = "ba-TA"

Read the following combinations 2 times:

B9 בַּתָ שַׁת תָת תְשָׁ בְּשָׁ

B10 * Example with three letters and two vowels: בַּתָשׁ = "ba-TASH"

B11 בַּתָשׁ שָׁבַשׁ תָתָשׁ בַּתָשׁ שַׁבָּת
_{See Lesson Fill-Ins}

C - Roots

Word Meaning	Key Word	Root Meaning	Root
Sabbath	שַׁבָּת	rest, stop	ש.ב.ת

C1

Most Hebrew words are built from three letters (sometimes 2) called a **ROOT**	C2
Middle and bottom dots and vowels are not written in roots	C3
Words from the same root share similar meanings	C4
Vowels, prefixes and suffixes change the meaning Example: שַׁבָּתוֹן (sha-ba-TON) means "sabbatical"	C5

C6 Circle the Hebrew root for "rest/stop" in the following Scripture:
(Remember that there may be extra letters before or after the root.)

זָכוֹר אֶת־יוֹם הַשַּׁבָּת לְקַדְּשׁוֹ.

za-KHOR et-yom ha-sha-BAT l-kad-SHO

Remember the Sabbath day to keep it holy. (see Exodus 20:8)

שַׁבָּת

C7 *Exodus 31:13 tells us that keeping the Shabbat (Sabbath) on the seventh day is a sign of the covenant between Adonai (God) and those who love Him. The Shabbat is one of His "mo-a-DEEM" (appointed times). Just as He rested on the seventh day after creation, He has asked us to honor His commandment to take a day of rest. His blessings will follow!*

Hebrew with Joy!   Lesson 1   ב ת ש

Write each letter or vowel three times in block or script then <u>make a flashcard</u> to help you:

D - Writing

**Script	Practice then make flashcards	Block	Letter	
כּ		בּ	בּ	D1
e		שׁ	שׁ	D2
ת		ת	ת	D3
		ָ ַ		D4

↑ **Normally, vowels and dots are not written in script.   D5

שַׁבָּת   Write the Hebrew word for "Sabbath" (including the vowels) then make a   D6
flashcard for the key word *and* the root:

Lesson 1 ב ת ש   Hebrew with Joy!

Name _____   # Exercises Lesson 1

Read the following letter combinations two times: ⬅

1. בַּ שָׁ שַׁ תָשׁ בַּת תָת בָּתְשׁ שַׁבָּת

Practice writing each letter and vowel combination ten times in block or script:

2. בַּ
3. שָׁ
4. תָ

Circle the letters that make the same sound as the letters on the far right:

5. שַׁת ⬅ בַּת תָשׁ ש̣ת בְּשׁ תָת (שַׁת) שָׁב
6. בַּת ⬅ בַּת תָשׁ שַׁת בְּשׁ תָת שַׁת שָׁב בַּת
7. תָת ⬅ בַּת תָת שַׁת בְּשׁ תָת שָׁב בָּת תָת
8. בְּב ⬅ בַּת תָת שָׁת בַּב תָת שַׁת שָׁב בְּב

9. Write the Hebrew word for "Sabbath" 3 times:

_____   _____   _____
_____   _____   _____

10. In **Sephardic** Hebrew, which syllable usually receives the accent? Circle the correct answer:

First   Middle   Second-to-Last   Last

11. Write Hebrew letters and vowels that have the same sound as the following English words:

_____ shot   _____ bought   תָת תָת taught

12. Make your own flashcards by writing each new letter and vowel on one side of a notecard and its sound on the other side. Then practice until they are memorized.

Hebrew with Joy!   Lesson 1   ש ת ב

Exercises Lesson 1

13. What is the meaning of the Hebrew **ROOT** שׁ.ב.ת ?

_____

14. Circle the word for "Sabbath" in the following Scripture - Exodus 20:8:

זָכוֹר אֶת־יוֹם הַשַּׁבָּת לְקַדְּשׁוֹ.

15. Write the English translation of Exodus 20:8:

_____

16. Circle the roots for "rest/stop" in Isaiah 58:13-14:

אִם־תָּשִׁיב מִשַּׁבָּת רַגְלֶךָ עֲשׂוֹת חֲפָצֶיךָ בְּיוֹם קָדְשִׁי וְקָרָאתָ
לַשַּׁבָּת עֹנֶג לִקְדוֹשׁ יְהוָה מְכֻבָּד וְכִבַּדְתּוֹ מֵעֲשׂוֹת דְּרָכֶיךָ
מִמְּצוֹא חֶפְצְךָ וְדַבֵּר דָּבָר:

אָז תִּתְעַנַּג עַל־יְהוָה וְהִרְכַּבְתִּיךָ עַל־בָּמֳתֵי/ "עַל־בָּמֳתֵי"
אָרֶץ וְהַאֲכַלְתִּיךָ נַחֲלַת יַעֲקֹב אָבִיךָ כִּי פִּי יְהוָה דִּבֵּר:

17. *In your own words,* (in English) summarize Isaiah 58:13-14:

_____
_____
_____
_____
_____
_____
_____

Hebrew with Joy!

Lesson 2   ל מ ם

Israeli Phrases
Nice to meet you!   na-EEM m-OD!
See you later!   l-heet-ra-OT!

A - Letters

Sound	Name	Letter	
"l" as in light	**LA**-med	ל	A1
"m" as in molehill	Mem	מ	A2
"m" as in molehill	Mem so-FEET* *(used at the end of a word)*	ם	A3

* so-FEET = "Final"- Mem is one of five Hebrew letters that change their form at the end of a word.   A4

Read each line two times:

A5   מַב תֵל מֵם תַם בָ מַ תָ לָ שָ

A6   שָׁם שַׁבָּת מֵתָשׁ מָלֵם תַם לָם בַּם   there

A7   During **Chanukah**, the Feast of Dedication, the traditional **dreidel** (spinning top) game is played. In America, the four Hebrew letters on the dreidel stand for the words "A Great Miracle Happened THERE." שׁ stands for "there" – from the word שָׁם (sham). But, in Israel, this letter changes to a פ. Then, they stand for "A Great Miracle happened HERE!" (Po פֹה)

B - Vowels

Sound	Vowel	
"o" as in "over" (dot is **O**VER the letter)	וֹ	B1
	ֹ	B2

Read each line two times:

B3   תוֹת שֹׁת בּוֹם לֹם ת שֹׁ מוֹ ל שׁוּ

B4   שָׁלוֹם תוֹלָם שְׁמוֹ תּוֹשׁ מוֹת שָׁם

21

Lesson 2   ל מ ם   *Hebrew with Joy!*

Write each letter or vowel three times in block or script then *make a flashcard* to help you study:

Script	Practice then make a flashcard	Block	Letter	
ℓ		ל	ל	C1
N		מ	מ	C2
ρ		ם	ם	C3
ו		ו	וֹ	C4

C - Writing

Word Meaning	Key Word	Root Meaning	Root	
peace, hello, goodbye	שָׁלוֹם	completion, wholeness	ש.ל.ם	D1
At times, extra letters may be added between root letters. For instance, in שָׁלוֹם, the ו is added				D2

D - Root

"Jerusalem" (y-roo-sha-**LAI**-yeem in Hebrew) comes from the root ש.ל.ם
   y-roo= they will see
   sha-lem = peace, wholeness, completion, and perfection
   sha-**LAI**-yeem= "**LAI**-yeem" ending means <u>double</u> shalom!

D3

Circle the words for "peace" in the following scripture:

יֵצֶר סָמוּךְ תִּצֹּר שָׁלוֹם שָׁלוֹם   D4

YE-tser sa-**MOOKH** tee-**TSOR** sha-**LOM** sha-**LOM**

You keep in perfect peace one whose mind is stayed on You.   (Isaiah 26:3)

Write the Key Word (include the vowels) then make a flashcard for the key word *and* the root:

שָׁלוֹם ------------------------------   D5

You can now read the following beloved Sabbath greeting: שַׁבָּת שָׁלוֹם!   D6

22

Paleo-Hebrew
The letters we are studying today have evolved over the centuries. Originally, the **Paleo-Hebrew** letters represented pictures with special meanings.
(For more study, search online for Ancient Hebrew, Picto-Hebrew or Paleo Hebrew)

"Shalom" study by Dr. I Suuquina:

ם	ו	ל	שׁ	Modern Letter
∿∿	Y	⌒	⊔⊔	Ancient Letter
water	nail	staff	teeth	Letter Meaning
chaos	attach	authority	destroy	Deeper Meaning

Shalom: **Destroying** the **authority attached** to **chaos**.

For more resources by Dr. I. Suuquina, check out their website:
http://www.indigenousmessengers.com

Lesson 2　ל מ　　　　　　　　　　　　　　　　　　　　　　　　*Hebrew with Joy!*

Slap Game: *If you are studying in a group, one person reads a combination, then, two other people try to be the first to **slap** that combination (or say the square number.) After reading all the combinations, rotate so there is a new reader. If you are studying by yourself, read each combination two times.*

4	3	2	1
מֶלֶשׁ	שֵׁם	בַּשׁ	מוֹת
8	**7**	**6**	**5**
לֹם	תַּת	לָתָשׁ	תוֹם
12	**11**	**10**	**9**
לוֹמֶת	מַלְת	שָׁלוֹם	בוֹת
16	**15**	**14**	**13**
לָלְת	שַׁבָּת	שׁוֹת	מוֹל

Hebrew with Joy!   Lesson 2   ל מ ם

Name _____   Exercises Lesson 2

.1   Read the following letter combinations three times:

לֹת מוֹת תֵּל שָׁם שַׁבָּת שְׁמוּ תוֹלָם שָׁלוֹם

Practice writing each letter and vowel combination ten times in block or script:

.2   לָ

.3   מַ

.4   מוֹ

.5   וֹ

Write 2 *different* Hebrew combinations that sound like each English word (include vowels):
(Remember to use the right form of Mem)

.6 Tom   תַּם   תָּם   .9 Mom

.7 mole   .10 mall

.8 ball   .11 boat

.12   Circle the words for "peace" in Isaiah 26:3:

יֵצֶר סָמוּךְ תִּצֹּר שָׁלוֹם שָׁלוֹם כִּי בְךָ בָּטוּחַ׃

.13   Write the English meaning of Isaiah 26:3:

_____

_____

.14   Write the Hebrew words for "Sabbath peace" two times (include vowels):

25

Exercises Lesson 2

15. What is the meaning of the Hebrew root שׁ.ל.ם ?

_____

Circle the root letters שׁ.ל.ם in the following words:

16. לְשַׁלֵּם — to pay/complete a transaction (l-sha-LEM)

17. שְׁלֹמֹה — Solomon/man of peace (**SHLO**-mo)

18. יְרוּשָׁלַיִם — Jerusalem/city of peace (y-roo-sha-**LAI**-yeem)

19. מֻשְׁלָם — complete/perfect (moo-SHLAM)

20. רְפוּאָה שְׁלֵמָה — complete healing (r-foo-AH shle-MA)

21. Circle the words for "peace" (eight times) in this traditional Hebrew prayer, Oseh Shalom:

עוֹשֶׂה שָׁלוֹם בִּמְרוֹמָיו הוּא יַעֲשֶׂה שָׁלוֹם עָלֵינוּ
וְעַל כָּל יִשְׂרָאֵל, וְאִמְרוּ, וְאִמְרוּ: אָמֵן
יַעֲשֶׂה שָׁלוֹם, יַעֲשֶׂה שָׁלוֹם, שָׁלוֹם עָלֵינוּ וְעַל כָּל יִשְׂרָאֵל
יַעֲשֶׂה שָׁלוֹם, יַעֲשֶׂה שָׁלוֹם, שָׁלוֹם עָלֵינוּ וְעַל כָּל יִשְׂרָאֵל

22. Look up this Hebrew prayer (Oseh Shalom) on the internet and write the English translation:

_____

_____

_____

23. By yourself or with a partner, use your flashcards to practice the sounds of the letters and vowels in Lessons 1 and 2. Make sure that you know them before starting Lesson 3!

Hebrew with Joy!   Lesson 3   ר י ה

Lesson 3   ר י ה

Israeli Greetings

BO-ker tov (good morning)   **E**-rev tov (good evening)   **LAI**-la tov (good night)   sha-**VOO**-a tov (good week)

A - Letters

Sound	Name	Letter	
"**r**" as in **r**est (This is a "guttural" sound made in the back of the throat)	Raysh	ר	A1
"**y**" as in **y**es	Yud/Yod	י	A2
"**h**" as in **h**oly or **silent** at the end of a word (Hay has a **h**ole!)	Hay	ה	A3

The open space in the ה is like a door - no matter how far we've strayed, Adonai always leaves a way, a space, an opening for turning back to Him!   A4

Read each line two times and translate the words on the second line:

רַ רְ הָ יָ הוֹ רַָה יְה שֶׁר תוֹר יַר   A5

הַר מַה יָה מוֹרָה יוֹם תּוֹרָה   A6
mountain   what   ____   teacher (f)   ____   ____   A7

*The dot inside the ת does not change the letter sound.   A8
Only three Hebrew letters change their sound when a dot is added inside: פ כ ב
(With the dot, the letter has a harder sound)
To remember the three letters, think of the sounds in "backpack:" B.K.P.K.

Lesson 3   רי ה   *Hebrew with Joy!*

B - Roots

Word Meaning	Key Word	Root Meaning	Root	
Instruction, teaching, law, first five books of the Bible	תּוֹרָה	hit the mark	י.ר.ה	B1
	In some words, one or more of the root letters drop. For instance, in תּוֹרָה, the י drops			B2

Circle the Hebrew word for "instruction" (first and last root letters drop!):

שָׁלוֹם רָב לְאֹהֲבֵי תוֹרָתֶךָ   B3

sha-LOM rav l-o-ha-VAY to-ra-TE-kha

Great peace have those who love Your instruction..   Psalm 119:165

Jewish scholars use a style of study called a **MIDRASH** - an intense, sometimes loud and lively group study of the Torah. Jews believe that "Torah instruction and knowledge is not gained except in the company of others." What a blessing that we also have the **ROO**-akh ha-**KO**-desh (Holy Spirit) to teach us!	B4

C - Writing

Script	Practice then make flashcards	Block	Letter	
ר		ר	ר	C1
י		י	י	C2
ה		ה	ה	C3

Write the key word meaning "instruction" (include the vowels) then make a flashcard for the key word *and* the root:

-- תּוֹרָה   C4

Hebrew with Joy!   Lesson 3   ה י ר

D - Vowels

Sound	Vowel	
"e" as in egg (as in two eggs in a basket)	ֶ	D1
"e" as in egg (as in three eggs in a basket)	ֱ	D2
"e" as in egg (as in five eggs in a basket)	ֵ	D3

Make flashcards for the vowels above: D4

Read the combinations two times:

שֵׁם   שֶׁל   הֵם   בֵּל   יֶל   רֶם   הַר   D5
_____

When the ֶ *appears twice (side-by-side) the first one is accented* as in **SHE**-mesh   שֶׁמֶשׁ   D6

הַשֵׁם   מוֹרֶה   מֹשֶׁה   שֶׁמֶשׁ   D7

_____   teacher (m)   _____   sun   D8

Sometimes, two letters share the same dot: מֹשֶׁה   D9

E - Prefix הַ

Use the prefix הַ to add "the" before a Hebrew word:
Note: sometimes a dot is added in the letter following the הַ.   E1

the = הַ   *the name* = הַשֵׁם

Read each word then write the English translation of the following: E2

הַתּוֹרָה   הַשַׁבָּת   הַשָׁלוֹם

_____   _____   _____

"The ability of the הַ to add individuality and character to a word is indicative of what also happens to any person when the Holy Spirit is breathed into their lives...they progress from being just "a" person to being "the" person God has made in His own image."   E3
In His Own Words by L. Grant Luton p.63

Lesson 3 ריה *Hebrew with Joy!*

Lesson 3 -Board Game: *Each player or team needs a different marker. With a partner or by yourself, roll a die and move forward the number on the die. Each time you land on a word, read it and try to translate:*

Start → שֵׁם → שֵׁם → יָד → בַּת → מָה → יוֹם → הַר → מֹשֶׁה → Back to Start → מוֹרָה → מוֹרָה → שָׁלוֹם → שַׁבָּת → הַשֵּׁם → תּוֹרָה → הַתּוֹרָה → הַשַּׁבָּת → שֶׁמֶשׁ → Winner!

Hebrew with Joy!   Lesson 3   ה י ר

Exercises Lesson 3   שֵׁם _____

Read aloud two times and translate these Hebrew words:

1. מֹשֶׁה שֶׁמֶשׁ הַר הַשֵּׁם בַּת תּוֹרָה שָׁלוֹם שַׁבָּת

Using numbers, match the Hebrew phrases to their meaning:

2. l-heet-ra-OT	___My name is …	6. **BO**-ker tov	___Good evening
3. na-EEM m-OD	_4_ Hello	7. sha-**VOO**-a tov	___Good week
4. שָׁלוֹם	___See you later!	8. **LAI**-la tov	___Good morning
5. sh-mee	___Nice to meet you	9. **E**-rev tov	___Good night

Practice writing each combination 10 times in block or script:

10. ךְ
11. הַ
12. רִ

Circle the Hebrew letters that sound like the English words:

13. hall → הֵל (הַל) (הָל) תַל הוֹל הַל הֵל
14. bet → בֵּת בַּת בֵּה בֶּה בּוֹה בֵּה בַּת
15. yet → יוֹת יֵת יֶת יוֹת רֶת יַת יְה
16. home → הֵם תוֹם הֹם הֶם תוֹם הוֹם

17. Write the following words in Hebrew (include vowels):

      instruction   peace   Sabbath   the name

31

Lesson 3 ה י ר Hebrew with Joy!

Exercises Lesson 3

18. Circle the word for "instruction" in the Hebrew Scripture Jeremiah 31:32(33):

נָתַתִּי אֶת־תּוֹרָתִי בְּקִרְבָּם וְעַל־לִבָּם אֶכְתֲּבֶנָּה

19. Fill in the missing English word:
"I will put My _____ within them and write it on their heart"   Jeremiah 31:32(33)

20. Write the meaning of the Hebrew **ROOT** י.ר.ה ?

_____

Write the English names of the five books of the תּוֹרָה below (**Note**: They are not in order!):
You may want to search the internet for "Hebrew names of the books of the Bible"

English Name	Meaning of the Hebrew Name	Transliteration	Hebrew Name	
	In the desert/wilderness	ba-meed-BAR	בְּמִדְבַּר	.21
	And He called	va-yeek-RA	וַיִּקְרָא	.22
Genesis	In the beginning	b-re-SHEET	בְּרֵאשִׁית	.23
	Names	sh-MOT	שְׁמוֹת	.24
	Words/Things	d-va-REEM	דְּבָרִים	.25

Being called up to recite the Torah blessing during a service is considered a great honor!
In Hebrew, this is called making "Aliyah" = meaning "to go up".

26. Circle the words for "instruction" in this Hebrew prayer that is chanted before reading the Torah:

בָּרוּךְ אַתָּה יְהוָה אֱלֹהֵינוּ מֶלֶךְ הָעוֹלָם אֲשֶׁר בָּחַר בָּנוּ מִכָּל הָעַמִּים
וְנָתַן לָנוּ אֶת תּוֹרָתוֹ. בָּרוּךְ אַתָּה יְהוָה נוֹתֵן הַתּוֹרָה.

Blessed are You, LORD our God, King of the universe, who has chosen us from among all the nations and given us His Torah. Blessed are You LORD, giver of the Torah.

Hebrew with Joy!   Lesson 4   נ ע | א

Lesson 4   נ ן ע א

> **Israeli Greetings**
> How's it going?   ma neesh-MA?
> Good, thanks!   tov, to-DA!

A - Letters

Sound	Name	Letter	
"n" as in **n**ame	Nun	נ	A1
"n" as in **n**ame	Nun so-FEET (Final Nun)	ן	A2
Silent (takes the vowel sound)	**AY**-in	ע	A3
Silent (takes the vowel sound)	**A**-lef	א	A4

> א *is the first letter of the Hebrew Alef-Bet so it has a number value of "one." (e-KHAD)*
> א *represents the Holy "One" of Israel and is also the first letter in these names of God:*
>   *e-lo-HEEM* אֱלֹהִים *(God) and a-do-NAI* אֲדֹנָי *(my master)*

A5

Read each line twice and translate the words on the second line:

אַ ע אוֹ נוּ אֶל עַן נת רֶן מֶן יִן   A6

אֶל עַם אַתָּה אוֹר בֶּן אַבָּא אָמֵן   A7
____ people you (ms) light ___ ___ ___   A8

B - Writing

Script	Practice then make flashcards	Block	Letter	
ﬀ		נ	נ	B1
׀		ן	ן	B2
ᵹ		ע	ע	B3
IC		א	א	B4

33

Lesson 4 נ ע | א   Hebrew with Joy!

C - Vowels

	Vowel	Sound
C1	◌ִ	"ee" as in "feet" — The vowel is under the letter's feet!
C2	◌ִי	"ee" as in "feet" (The Yud in a vowel has the "ee" sound)

C3   Make flashcards for the vowels above:

Read this line 2 times:

C4   הִ   עִי   תְא   לִים   יְן   בִּין   אֲנִי   _____ I

	Vowel	Sh-va	Sound
C5	◌ְ	Sh-va	Silent or short "uh" as in upon (one dot is upon the other!)

Sh-va Examples

	Word	Vowels	Description
C6	שְׁמַע	◌ְ ◌ַ	At the **beginning of a word**, the short "uh" sound
C7	לְהִתְרָאוֹת	◌ְ ◌ִ ◌ְ ◌ָ	In the **middle of a word**, usually stops a syllable and is silent (If there are two Sh-vas side by side, the first is silent, the second has the short "uh" sound)
C8	אַתְּ	◌ַ ◌ְ	At the **end of a word**: always silent

C9   Make a flashcard for the sh-va:

Read this line two times:

C10   עִית   תְשׁ   נֵר   לֶם   מְא   נְשׁ   אַתְּ you (fs)

Read this line two times then translate:

C11   לְהִתְרָאוֹת   מְנוֹרָה   שְׁלֹמֹה   בְּרִית
C12   _____   _____   _____   covenant

C13   The בְּרִית מִילָה "covenant of circumcision" takes place on the eighth day of a Jewish boy's life when he is also given his name! (see Leviticus 12:3) An Israeli tradition is to take the baby's foreskin, bury it in the yard and plant a new tree right above, signifying new life!

Hebrew with Joy!   Lesson 4   נ | ע א

Read this line two times then translate:

שְׁמַע	הַבָּא	אֱלֹהִים	C14
_____	the one who comes	_____	C15

D - Root

Word Meaning	Key Word	Root Meaning	Root	
hear! listen!	שְׁמַע	hear and obey	שׁ.מ.ע	D1

Circle the word for "hear" in Deuteronomy 6:4:

שְׁמַע יִשְׂרָאֵל יְהוָה אֱלֹהֵינוּ יְהוָה אֶחָד: D2

sh-MA yees-ra-EL a-do-NAI e-lo-**HAY**-noo a-do-NAI e-KHAD

Hear (O) Israel, The LORD our God, the LORD is one.

Note: יְהוָה means "the LORD" and can be pronounced "a-do-NAI."

The שְׁמַע Sh'ma (Deuteronomy 6:4), is the most beloved prayer in Judaism, recited three times a day by religiously observant Jews. It is found in the mezuzah (prayer box on the doorposts) along with these Scriptures: Deuteronomy 6:5-9 and 11:13-21
Inside the Phylacteries (leather prayer boxes wrapped around the arm and forehead) are these scriptures: Deuteronomy 6:4-9, 11:13-21, Exodus 13:1-10, 11-16.   D3

_____   Write the Hebrew word for "hear" and make a flashcard for the key word *and* the root (Don't forget the vowels!):   D4

Tic Tac Toe

Before starting the game, make ten game pieces – five of one color and five of another. Each player picks a color. To play the game, one player puts a piece down on a square and must read and translate the word. Then the opponent plays. The object is to be the first to have three pieces of their color in a row (vertical, horizontal or diagonal).

שָׁלוֹם	תּוֹרָה	אַבָּא
אֱלֹהִים	שְׁמַע	הַבָּא
הַשֵּׁם	שַׁבָּת	בְּרִית

Hebrew with Joy!   Lesson 4   נ ע | א

Exercises Lesson 4

שֵׁם _____

Read and translate these words:

1. אֶל   עַם   אוֹר   אַבָּא   אָמֵן   שַׁבָּת   תּוֹרָה   שְׁמַע   שָׁלוֹם

Using numbers, match the Hebrew words to their meaning:

2. אַתָּה	___hear	6. tov to-DA	___good morning
3. בֵּן	___Dad	7. **BO**-ker tov	___how are you
4. אַבָּא	___son	8. **LAI**-la tov	___good, thanks
5. שְׁמַע	_2_ you (masc)	9. ma neesh-MA	___good night

Translate the English words into Hebrew letters in the puzzle below – DON'T USE VOWELS!

	ן	מ c	א
		b	
			a
	d		

.10 amen
.11 peace
.12 hear
.13 instruction

Notice the small letters (a,b,c,d) in the squares of the puzzle above.
Copy the Hebrew letter from those squares to the line below:

14. a_____ b_____ c _מ_ d_____

15. What is the English name for the king in line 14? _____

Write the correct form of the Nun in the following words from the lesson then translate to English:

16. אֲנִי I_____ אָמֵ☐ _____ מ☐וֹרָה _____

17. Practice writing each new combination four times:

נְ	אֵן	עִי
-------	-------	-------

Exercises Lesson 4

18. Write the English translation of the Sh'ma: (Deuteronomy 6:4)

Hebrew	שְׁמַע יִשְׂרָאֵל יְהֹוָה אֱלֹהֵינוּ יְהֹוָה אֶחָד׃
English	

19. What is the meaning of the Hebrew root שׁ.מ.ע ?

_____

Most English Bibles break **Psalm 119** into sections.
Open a bible that does this and answer the following questions:

20. Which English translation did you use? _____

21. How many sections are in Psalm 119? _____

22. How many verses are in each section? _____

23. How are the sections named? _____

24. What is the name of the first section? _____

25. What is the name of the last section? _____

26. Do you have a favorite verse from Psalm 119? If so, which verse? _____

Write the English meaning for the following words from the lesson which all start with א.

27. אַבָּא _____

28. אֱלֹהִים _____

29. אֶחָד _____ (Hint – from the Sh'ma)

Hebrew with Joy!   Lesson 5 ח ך כ

Lesson 5   כ ך ח

> **Israeli Greetings**
> How's it going?   ma neesh-MA?
> OK/fine   b-**SE**-der

A - Letters

Sound	Name	Letter	
"**kh**" as in Ba**ch** (This is a "guttural" sound made in the back of the throat)	Kaf (without a dot) (BKPK letter - no dot softens the sound)	כ	A1
	Kaf so-FEET* (Final Kaf)	ך	A2
	Khet	ח	A3

*Kaf so-FEET has two forms : ךְ "kh" or ךָ "kha"   A4

> ח represents "life" (khai-YEEM) חַיִּים. It is common for Jewish women to wear a חַי (khai - "live") necklace to represent the incredible importance of *life* to the Jewish people. From the Passover story in Exodus 12:22-23, the doorposts that the angel of death passed over (providing life) were in the shape of a ח.   A5

Read the following line two times:

A6   כַ   ח   כוּ   כֹת   חֶן   אַךְ   לֵךְ   לָךְ

Read and then translate:

A7   רָחֵל _____   לֶחֶם _bread_   מֶלֶךְ _____

B - Writing

Script	Practice then make flashcards	Block	Letter	
כ		כ	כ	B1
ך		ך	ך	B2
ח		ח	ח	B3

Lesson 5 ח ך כ   *Hebrew with Joy!*

C – Look-Alike Letters

כָ נָ	Kaf is wider	C4	הָ חָ	Hay has a hole	C1
רָ דָ	Raysh is shorter	C5	בָּ כָּ	Bet has a bottom bar. Both can have dots!	C2
דָ ךָ	Kaf SoFEET is longer	C6	תָ חָ	Tav has a toe!	C3

Read the following line two times:

C7   לְךָ   לָךְ   נוֹת   כוֹת   בֵּן   כֵּן   לֹח   לֵת   בֵּה   בֵּח

D - Vowels

Sound	Vowel	
"oo" as in "too" ("oo - it hurts!")	וּ	D1
	ֻ	D2

D3   Make flashcards for the vowels above:

Read the following line two times:

D4   רָעֵךְ   חוּשִׁי   לוּד   בֻּ   נֻם   מֻ   רוּ   כוּ

Read the following line two times, then translate the words:

D5   בָּרוּךְ   יְשׁוּעָה   אֱמוּנָה   הַלְלוּיָהּ   רוּת

D6   _____   salvation   faith   _____   _____

Hebrew with Joy!   Lesson 5 כ ך ח

E - Root

Word Meaning	Key Word	Root Meaning	Root
blessed	בָּרוּךְ	bless, kneel	ב.ר.ך

E1

E2   בְּרָכָה   Blessing or Benediction

E3   בֶּרֶךְ   Knee (bow the knee)

E4   בָּרוּךְ הַבָּא   Blessed is the comer - Welcome! (to one person) / Used to greet a new baby

E5   בְּרוּכִים הַבָּאִים   Blessed are the comers - Welcome! (to a group) / Wedding greeting for a new couple

E6   If you see this sign, you are on Hwy 1 driving into Jerusalem. What does the sign say?

E7   Write the Hebrew word for "blessed" then make a flashcard for the key word *and* the root:

E8   בָּרוּךְ הַבָּא בְּשֵׁם יְהוָה.

ba-ROOKH ha-BA b-SHEM a-do-NAI

Blessed is the one who comes in the name of the LORD. Psalm 118:26

E9   יְהוָה means "the LORD" and can be pronounced "a-do-NAI."

E10

...בָּרוּךְ אַתָּה יְהוָה

"Blessed are you, Adonai..." These beloved words begin many Jewish prayers, a testimony to the reverence and devotion belonging to Adonai alone. Many of these prayers are included in Jewish holidays (mo-a-DEEM) - appointments with God. Every Friday evening at sundown, Jewish homes around the world celebrate the beginning of Shabbat by reciting these prayers: Lighting the Shabbat Candles, Blessing the Bread and Blessing the Wine. On the following pages, you can practice these prayers and experience your own Shabbat celebration.

Hebrew with Joy!   Lesson 5 כ ך ח

Shabbat שַׁבָּת

Exodus 20:8-11 *"Remember Yom Shabbat [day of Shabbat] to keep it holy. You are to work six days, and do all your work, but the seventh day is a Shabbat to Adonai your God. In it you shall not do any work... For in six days Adonai made heaven and earth, the sea, and all that is in them, and rested on the seventh day. Thus Adonai blessed Yom Shabbat, and made it holy."*

Isaiah 58:13-14 *"If you turn back your foot from Shabbat, from doing your pleasure on My holy day, and call Shabbat a delight, the holy day of Adonai honorable, if you honor it, not going your own ways, not seeking your own pleasure, nor speaking your usual speech, then You will delight yourself in Adonai, and I will let you ride over the heights of the earth. I will feed you with the heritage of your father Jacob."*

Candle Lighting Prayer
(new prayer from Exodus 20:8)

בָּרוּךְ אַתָּה יְהוָה אֱלֹהֵינוּ מֶלֶךְ הָעוֹלָם
אֲשֶׁר צִוָּנוּ לְכַבֵּד אֶת הַשַּׁבָּת וּלְקַדְּשָׁהּ. אָמֵן

ba-ROOKH a-TA a-do-NAI, e-lo-**HAY**-noo **ME**-lekh ha-o-LAM,
a-SHER tsee-**VA**-noo l-kha-BED et ha-sha-BAT ool-kad-SHA. *a-MEN*

*We praise You, Adonai our God, King of the universe,
who has commanded us to honor the Sabbath and to keep it holy. Amen*

HaMotsee (Who Brings Forth) - Blessing over the Bread

בָּרוּךְ אַתָּה יְהוָה אֱלֹהֵינוּ מֶלֶךְ הָעוֹלָם הַמּוֹצִיא לֶחֶם מִן הָאָרֶץ. אָמֵן

ba-ROOKH a-TA a-do-NAI, e-lo-**HAY**-noo **ME**-lekh ha-o-LAM, ha-**MO**-tsee **LE**-khem meen ha-**A**-rets. a-MEN
Blessed are You, Adonai our God, Ruler of the universe, who brings forth bread from the earth. Amen

Kiddush (Sanctification) - Blessing over the Wine

בָּרוּךְ אַתָּה יְהוָה אֱלֹהֵינוּ מֶלֶךְ הָעוֹלָם בּוֹרֵא פְּרִי הַגָּפֶן. אָמֵן.

ba-ROOKH a-TA a-do-NAI, e-lo-**HAY**-noo **ME**-lekh ha-o-LAM, bo-RE p-REE ha-**GA**-fen. *a-MEN*
Blessed are you, Adonai, our God, Ruler of the universe, creator of the fruit of the vine. Amen

Sh'ma

שְׁמַע יִשְׂרָאֵל יְהוָה אֱלֹהֵינוּ יְהוָה אֶחָד:
בָּרוּךְ שֵׁם כְּבוֹד מַלְכוּתוֹ לְעוֹלָם וָעֶד:

sh-MA yees-ra-EL a-do-NAI e-lo-**HAY**-noo a-do-NAI e-KHAD:
ba-ROOKH shem k-VOD mal-**KHOO**-to l-o-LAM va-ED.

*Hear (O) Israel, The LORD our God, the LORD is one.
Blessed is the name of His glorious kingdom for ever and ever.*

Family Blessings

For Sons:

May Adonai inspire you to love in the tradition of Abraham, Isaac and Jacob.
May you grow closer to Adonai, our LORD, in strength and dignity and shine His light to those around you!

For Daughters:

May Adonai inspire you to love in the tradition of Sarah and Rebekah, Rachel and Leah.
May you grow in the love of Adonai, our King, and be a light to the world!

Blessing the Parents: (by the children)

May God bless your love for one another and for us!

For the Wife (from Proverbs 31):

A woman of valor – who can find? She is to be valued above rubies. Her husband trusts in her, and so he lacks nothing. She does him good, never harm, all the days of her life. She reached out to those in need, and extends her hands to the poor. She is clothed in strength and dignity and she faces the future cheerfully. She speaks with wisdom: the law of kindness is on her lips. She shines with the love of Adonai to her family and in her community. Her children rise up and bless her; her husband sings her praises.

For the Husband (from Psalm 112):

Blessed is the man who fears and glorifies Adonai, who greatly delights in Adonai's commandments. The generation of the upright will be blessed. His household prospers, and his righteousness endures forever. Light shines in the darkness for the upright. For the one who is gracious, compassionate and just. He is not afraid of evil tidings; his mind is firm; trusting in Adonai. His heart is steady, he will not be afraid. He gives freely to the poor. His righteousness endures forever; his life is exalted in honor.

The Aaronic Blessing:

יְבָרֶכְךָ יְהוָה וְיִשְׁמְרֶךָ: יָאֵר יְהוָה פָּנָיו אֵלֶיךָ וִיחֻנֶּךָּ:
יִשָּׂא יְהוָה פָּנָיו אֵלֶיךָ וְיָשֵׂם לְךָ שָׁלוֹם:

y-va-**RE**-kh-kha a-do-**NAI** v-yeesh-m-**RE**-kha; ya-**ER** a-do-**NAI** pa-**NAV** e-**LE**-kha vee-khoo-**NE**-kha;
yee-**SA** a-do-**NAI** pa-**NAV** e-**LE**-kha v-ya-**SEM** l-**KHA** sha-**LOM**

*Adonai bless you and keep you! Adonai make His face to shine on you and be gracious to you!
Adonai turn his face to you and grant you shalom. Numbers 6:24-26*

Shabbat Shalom! שַׁבָּת שָׁלוֹם!

Hebrew with Joy!   Lesson 5   כ ך ח

Exercises Lesson 5

שֵׁם _____

1. Read aloud two times and translate these Hebrew words:

שָׁלוֹם   בָּרוּךְ   שְׁמַע   הַלְלוּיָהּ   מֶלֶךְ   תּוֹרָה   שַׁבָּת   הַשֵּׁם

Write in Hebrew the words below (include the vowels):

Hebrew	English	Hebrew	English
	5. the Name		2. peace
	6. hear		3. Sabbath
	7. king		4. instruction

8. Write the Hebrew word for "blessed" three times:

_____
_____

9. Practice writing each combination six times in block or script:

כִּ
דָ
חוּ

10. Write the English meaning:

בָּרוּךְ אַתָּה יְהוָה   _____

11. What are the two meanings of the Hebrew root ב.ר.ך ?

_____

12. This prayer is always chanted after the Sh'ma (Deuteronomy 6:4). Circle the word for "blessed":

בָּרוּךְ שֵׁם כְּבוֹד מַלְכוּתוֹ לְעוֹלָם וָעֶד:

ba-**ROOKH** shem k-VOD mal-**KHOO**-to l-o-LAM va-ED
Blessed is the name of His glorious kingdom for ever and ever.

13. Take the self-quiz on the next page (without looking up the answers.) Then, using your set of flashcards for lessons 1-5 *practice, practice, practice*!

45

Lesson 5 כ ך ח   *Hebrew with Joy!*

שֵׁם _____   # Self-quiz – Lesson 5

We are halfway through the course. *Complete this page **without** looking up the answers.*
Use your flashcards to practice those you answered incorrectly.

A. Match the letters to their sounds:

___ א   8. kh
___ מ   9. r
_11_ ת   10. silent
___ ר   11. t
___ שׁ   12. n
___ ד   13. m
___ ן   14. sh
___ י   15. y

B. Match the letters to their sounds:

___ ה   1. kh
___ ם   2. silent
___ נ   3. n
___ ח   4. b
___ ע   5. h
___ ל   6. l
___ ב   7. m

C. Match the words:

___ Hear   1.הַשֵּׁם
___ Blessed   2.שְׁמַע
___ Peace   3.בָּרוּךְ
___ Sabbath   4.שַׁבָּת
___ The Name   5.שָׁלוֹם
___ Instruction 6.תּוֹרָה

D. Match the sounds (numbers can be repeated):

___ תֻ   1. too
___ תוֹ   2. tah
___ תָ   3. toe
___ תוּ   4. tee
___ תֶ   5. teh
___ תִי   6. tuh
___ תַ
___ תְ
___ תֵ
___ תִ

*Answers on Lesson Fill-In page

שֵׁם _____ Extra Challenge - Lesson 5

14. On the Shabbat Guide in this lesson, practice reading all of the prayers in Hebrew. Use the transliterations to help you with letters you don't know!

15. Before a Sabbath meal, use the Shabbat Guide to "remember the Sabbath and keep it holy." Let everyone have a part in reading the Scriptures and prayers.
This handout is just a guide – feel free to add or change any part.
Also, feel free to make copies of the Shabbat Guide to use in the future.

16. After Shabbat, write down your impressions of the experience below:

_____
_____
_____
_____
_____
_____
_____
_____
_____
_____
_____
_____
_____
_____
_____

Lesson 6 ו ב ד

| Israeli Phrases | שָׁלוֹם |
| Hello/goodbye friends! | kha-ve-REEM! |

A - Letters

Sound	Name	Letter	
"d" as in **d**oor	**DA**-let	ד	A1
"v" as in **v**ictory	Bet (without a dot) (BKPK letter)	ב	A2
"v" as in **v**ictory or silent as a vowel	Vav	ו	A3

Vav ו has a "v" sound if there is a vowel under it or no vowel: וְ וָ וַ ו   A4

Vav ו is silent as part of a vowel if there is a dot inside or over it: וֹ וּ   A5

Read the following line two times:

וּ וֹ וַ וְ וָא בְּ דָ בִי וּ דִי וַד   A6

Read the following line and translate:

יְיָ/יְהוָה   לֵב   תּוֹדָה   דָּוִד   אָב   A7

LORD   heart   _____   _____   father   A8
see below

יְהוָה (or the abbreviation יְיָ) is called the "unpronounceable Name of God" and is found more than six thousand times in the Scriptures! The original Hebrew did not contain vowels; therefore, there is no way to know how the Name of God should be pronounced. Hence, religiously observant Jews say the name "a-do-NAI" (my LORD) when they are in synagogue or reading their prayer books and they say the name "ha-SHEM" (the Name) at all other times. Some of the other names said in English: The LORD, Jehovah, Yehovah, Yah, Yahweh   A9

The Hebrew name can also take many forms: יְהוָה   יְיָ   יהוה

Lesson 6　ד ב ו　　　　　　　　　　　　　　　　　　　　　　　　　　　　　　*Hebrew with Joy!*

Read the following line and translate:

A10　שׁוּב　שָׁבוּעוֹת　עִבְרִית　חֲבֵרִים

A11　turn/return　_____　_____　_____

B - Prefix וֹ

B1　The prefix וְ or וּ is used to add "and" before a Hebrew word: "and peace" = וְשָׁלוֹם

Read each word then write the English translation of the following:

B2　וְשָׁמַע _____　　　וּמֹשֶׁה _____

B3　*In ancient Hebrew (Paleo-Hebrew), the Vav was the shape of a hook (which has the ability to "hook" things together – just like the word "and.") In fact, Torah scribes start each column with a Vav, thus "hooking" the columns together.*

C - Look-Alike Letters

אוֹ אָן Vav is shorter	C3	בּ כּ Bet has a bottom bar	C2	ד ר Dalet has a top bar	C1

Read the following line two times:

C4　כּוּ בּוּ עוֹ עָן　רַן רוּ　דִי רִי　דֹחַ רֹה

D - Writing

	Letter	Block	Practice, then make flashcards	Script	
D1	ד	ד		ד	
D2	בּ	בּ		כּ	
D3	ו	ו		ו	

50

Hebrew with Joy! Lesson 6

E - Vowels

Sound	Vowel	
"a" as in all	ָ	E1
At the **beginning or middle of a word** - "kha" as in חַלָּה At the **end of a word** - "akh" as in רוּחַ (say the vowel first, then the letter)	חַ	E2

Make flashcards for the vowels above: E3

Read the following lines and translate:

E4 חַלָּה   נֹחַ   רוּחַ   אַהֲבָה   עֲבוֹדָה

E5 _____   Noah   _____   _____   work/serve/worship
              love

E6 מָשִׁיחַ   מוֹעֲדִים   רַחֲמִים   עֲלִיָה

E7 anointed one   _____   mercy/mercies   _____
                                              see below

עֲלִיָה

*Jeremiah 23:3 says "I will gather the remnant of My flock out of all the countries where I have driven them, and will bring them back to their folds, and they will be fruitful and multiply." Since the late 1800s, Jews around the world have felt drawn to "Make Aliyah," to immigrate to Israel, the promised Jewish homeland. The word "**Aliyah**," meaning "**going up**," is a picture of going up to Jerusalem! "Aliyah" is also the word used in Jewish synagogue services for the privilege of being asked to "go up" to the "Beema" (raised platform) to recite the Hebrew prayers before and after the Torah reading.* E8

Lesson 6 ד ב ו   *Hebrew with Joy!*

F - Root

Word Meaning	Key Word	Root Meaning	Root
love (noun)	אַהֲבָה	love	א.ה.ב

F1

F2 — Write the Hebrew word for "love" then make a flashcard for the key word *and* the root:

F3 — Circle the root for "love":

וְאָהַבְתָּ אֵת יְיָ אֱלֹהֶיךָ

v-a-**HAV**-ta et a-do-**NAI** e-lo-**HE**-kha

And you shall love the LORD your God… Deuteronomy 6:5

G – Sing!

Write the Hebrew or English translation for the following three words:

_____ לְהִתְרָאוֹת _____ חֲבֵרִים _____ Good bye   G1

G2 — On the internet, look up "Shalom Chaverim" on YouTube, then read and sing the Hebrew as you listen to this famous Israeli good-bye song!

שָׁלוֹם חֲבֵרִים!
שָׁלוֹם חֲבֵרִים!
שָׁלוֹם. שָׁלוֹם.
לְהִתְרָאוֹת! לְהִתְרָאוֹת!
שָׁלוֹם. שָׁלוֹם.

Hebrew with Joy! Lesson 6 ו ב ד

Exercises Lesson 6

שֵׁם ‎_____

Read and translate these words:

1. שְׁמַע תּוֹרָה אַהֲבָה שַׁבָּת יְהוָה בָּרוּךְ שָׁלוֹם

Write the matching number under the picture:

2. עֶרֶב
tov

3. שָׁלוֹם
kha-ve-REEM

4. **BO**-ker tov

5. שְׁמִי ‎____
na-EEM m-OD

6. **LAI**-la tov

7. שָׁבוּעַ
tov

8. Practice writing and saying each combination six times in block or script:

דְּו

בְּל

וְךָ

9. Write the Hebrew word for "love" three times:

10. Write the Hebrew (include vowels) for the following English words (all words are in the lesson):

____ Spirit   ____ father   ____ heart   ____ thanks

11. What is the meaning of the Hebrew root א.ה.ב?

_____

53

Exercises Lesson 6

12. Write 2 different Hebrew forms of the "unpronounceable" Name of God:
----------   ----------
----------   ----------

13. Write the English meaning below (in the lesson!): וְאָהַבְתָּ אֵת יְיָ אֱלֹהֶיךָ
_____

14. What does וּ or וְ mean at the beginning of a word? _____

15. Circle the letter וְ found at the beginning of four words in Deuteronomy 6:5-6:

וְאָהַבְתָּ אֵת יְהוָה אֱלֹהֶיךָ בְּכָל־לְבָבְךָ וּבְכָל־נַפְשְׁךָ
וּבְכָל־מְאֹדֶךָ: וְהָיוּ הַדְּבָרִים הָאֵלֶּה אָנֹכִי מְצַוְּךָ
הַיּוֹם עַל־לְבָבֶךָ:

And you shall love Adonai your God with all your heart and with all your soul and with all your strength. And these words which I am commanding you today [shall be] on your heart.

16. Underline the *root* letters for "love" in the above scripture.

17. Circle the seven key Hebrew words below: Sabbath, peace, love, instruction, hear, LORD, blessed. The words can be vertical, horizontal or diagonal.

נ	י	ן	ו	ר	ב	ם
ת	ה	ב	ה	א	ת	ךּ
כ	ח	ת	ד	ע	ה	שׁ
ךּ	ל	ב	י	ה	ו	בּ
ה	ר	כ	י	ו	ל	ת
מ	ד	ה	נ	ם	כ	ל
ע	ח	ר	שׁ	ע	מ	שׁ

Hebrew with Joy!   Lesson 7   פ ז צ ץ

Lesson 7   פּ ז צ ץ

Israeli Phrases
Thanks very much   תּוֹדָה רַבָּה
You're welcome   b-va-ka-SHA

A - Letters

Sound	Name	Letter	
"p" as in **p**ray	Pay (with a dot) (BKPK letter)	פּ	A1
"z" as in **z**eal	**ZA**-yin	ז	A2
"ts" as in roo**ts**	**TSA**-dee (looks like praying hands)	צ	A3
"ts" as in roo**ts**	**TSA**-dee so-FEET (looks like reaching to God!)	ץ	A4

Read the following line two times:

A5   צָ צַ וִץ פּ זִי פּ פֶה יָז זֶה <u>this/that</u> עֵץ <u>   </u>

Look-Alike Letters | עֵ צֵ | A6

Read the following line two times:

A7   עִיפּ צִיפּ עֵן צֵן צַם עַם

Read the following line and translate:

A8   מְזוּזָה   מִשְׁפָּחָה   פּוּרִים   צִיצִית

<u>   </u>   <u>family</u>   <u>   </u>   <u>fringes</u>   A9

A10   *When an Orthodox boy turns three years old, his hair is cut for the first time and he also receives his first צִיצִית. "Speak to Bnei-Yisrael. Say to them that they are to make for themselves tzitzit on the corners of their garments throughout their generations, and they are to put a blue cord on each tzitzit. It will be your own tzitzit—so whenever you look at them, you will remember all the mitzvot [commandments] of Adonai (Numbers 15:38-39)*

Lesson 7   פ צ ז ץ   Hebrew with Joy!

Read the following line and try to translate:

A11   צִיּוֹן _____   חֻפָּה wedding canopy   בַּר מִצְוָה see below _____

A12   The **Bar Mitzvah** (Son of the Commandment) is the traditional coming into adulthood for a Jewish boy on his thirteenth birthday. Girls celebrate their **Bat Mitzvah** (Daughter of the Commandment) on their twelfth birthday (thirteenth birthday in Reform Judaism). The ceremony includes reading a portion of the Torah that was read on the week they were born. This author had the privilege of celebrating her Bat Mitzvah at age 62 (50 years after the normal tradition!)

B - Vowels

Sound	Vowel	
"ai" as in p**ie** ("a" + "ee") (vowel is flat like a pie יַ)	יַ	B1
"ay" as in l**ay** ("e" + "ee") (the eggs .. lay side by side)	יֵ	B2

Make flashcards for the vowels above:

Read this line 2 times:

B3   בֵּי בֵי דַי דֵי לִי לַי חִי זַי זֵי צַי צֵי פֵּי פִּי

Read the following lines and translate:

B4   אֱלֹהֵינוּ _____   בְּנֵי sons/children (of)   שַׁדַּי almighty _____

B5   יְרוּשָׁלַיִם _____   לְחַיִּים _____   חַיִּים _____   חַי live

B6   _____

B7   For the Jewish people, life is everything! God has protected His people and allowed them to חַי today in their own land. Each Hebrew letter is assigned a number value (called **Gematria**.) Because the number value of the letters ח (8) plus י (10) = 18, Jews traditionally tithe in multiples of 18. In the synagogue, this giving is done in ts-da-KA (charity) boxes. In fact, if you want to plant a tree in Israel, each tree costs $18!

Hebrew with Joy! Lesson 7 פ צ ץ

> Many Jewish homes have a מְזוּזָה prayer box (literally - doorpost) next to their doors to honor the Holy Scriptures placed inside. (See Deuteronomy 6:9) Some have "שׁ" on the cover which stands for שַׁדַּי - meaning "Almighty" (literally - my breast) The letters שדי also represent three words meaning "Guardians of the Doors of Israel!" (shom-REEM d-la-TOT yees-ra-EL) שׁוֹמְרִים דְּלָתוֹת יִשְׂרָאֵל

B8

C - Root

Meaning	Key Word	Root Meaning	Root	
life	חַיִּים	live	ח.י.ה	C1

Circle the Hebrew words meaning "Tree of Life":

עֵץ־חַיִּים הִיא לַמַּחֲזִיקִים בָּהּ   C2

ets khai-EEM hee la-ma-kha-zee-KEEM ba

She is a tree of life to those who are strong in her.   Proverbs 3:18

D - Writing

Script	Practice, then write flashcards	Block	Letter	
ꝑ		פ	פ	D1
5		ז	ז	D2
3		צ	צ	D3
ϙ		ץ	ץ	D4

*In script, the end of **TSA**-dee so-FEET goes up*   D5

Write the Hebrew word for "life" and make a flashcard for the key word *and* the root: D6

Lesson 7 פ צ ץ Hebrew with Joy!

Vowel Slap Game: *If you are studying in a group, one person reads a vowel sound, then two other people try to be the first to SLAP (or point to) that combination. After reading all the vowels, rotate so there is a new reader. If you are studying by yourself, point to random vowels to practice.*

Vowel Board Game: *Each player or team uses a different marker. With a partner or by yourself, roll a die and move forward the number on the die. Each time you land on a square, read the vowel sound. Extra challenge – say a Hebrew word that includes that vowel.*

At end of word!

Hebrew with Joy!   Lesson 7   פ צ ז

_____ שֵׁם   **Exercises Lesson 7**

Read and translate these words:

1. יְיָ בָּרוּךְ תּוֹרָה אַהֲבָה שְׁמַע חַיִּים שָׁלוֹם

2. Complete your letter, vowel and key word flashcards through lesson 7. Memorize all letters, vowels and key words before moving to the next lesson.

3. Write the missing Hebrew or English words:

	Hebrew	English
.4		almighty
.5	יְרוּשָׁלַיִם	
.6	בַּר מִצְוָה	
.7		live
.8	עֵץ חַיִּים	
.9		family

10. Practice reading and writing each combination six times in block or script:

צַר _____

עֵץ _____

זֵר _____

פֵּר _____

11. Write the correct form of the **TSA**-dee in the following words from the lesson and write the English translation:

_____ בַּר מִ□וָה _____ עֵ□ _____ □יּוֹן

59

Exercises Lesson 7

12. What is the meaning of the Hebrew root ח.י.ה?

_____

13. Write three Hebrew words that come from the root above:

------------------- ------------------- -------------------
------------------- ------------------- -------------------

14. This beloved Hebrew prayer based on Proverbs 3:17-18 is found In the Siddur (Jewish prayer book.) Circle the words for "tree of life" and "peace:"

עֵץ חַיִּים הִיא לַמַּחֲזִיקִים בָּהּ וְתֹמְכֶיהָ מְאֻשָּׁר
דְּרָכֶיהָ דַרְכֵי נֹעַם וְכָל נְתִיבוֹתֶיהָ שָׁלוֹם
הֲשִׁיבֵנוּ יהוה אֵלֶיךָ וְנָשׁוּבָה. חַדֵּשׁ יָמֵינוּ כְּקֶדֶם

"She is a tree of life to those who are strong in her and those who hold her fast will prosper [go straight] . Her ways are pleasant, and all of her paths peaceful."
(The last Hebrew line above is added in the Siddur, the Hebrew Prayer Book -
"Return us to you, God, so that we shall return; renew our days as of old.")

15. In your own words, summarize Proverbs 3:13-18:

_____
_____
_____
_____

16. In the Scripture above, who is "she"? (Hint – see Proverbs 3:13):

_____

Hebrew with Joy!

Lesson 8   פ ף ק כ

Sound	Name	Letter	
"f" as in **f**aith	Pay (BKPK -without a dot - soft sound)	פ	A1
"f" as in **f**aith	Pay so-FEET	ף	A2
"k" as in **k**ing	Koof	ק	A3
"k" as in **k**ing	Kaf (BKPK– with a dot - hard sound)	כ	A4

A - Letters

Israeli Phrases
All the honor/glory! (Well done!)   kol ha-ka-VOD!

Read the following lines two times:

A5   כַּיף   כִּיק   עַף   כִּיף   קוּ   קוֹ   פַּ   פֶּ

A6   כִּי   פּוּק   כִּין   עוּק   שִׁיךְ   לוּף   הַם   צֶךְ

Read the following lines and try to translate:

A7   שׁוֹפָר   קְהִילָה   צְדָקָה   נֶפֶשׁ   כָּבוֹד
A8   _____   community/congregation   charity   soul   honor/glory

A9   חֲנֻכָּה   תְּפִלָּה   יוֹם כִּפּוּר   הַתִּקְוָה
A10   _____   prayer   _____   see below

A11   הַתִּקְוָה *(The Hope) was a poem written in 1878, inspired by the Zionist movement (Jews returning to the Promised Land). It was not until 2004 that the Israeli government officially designated* הַתִּקְוָה *as Israel's national anthem. Today, this song is sung with tears of joy because, after centuries,* יְהוָה *has brought His chosen people home to freedom! Psalm 37:9 promises that "those who* **hope** *in the LORD will inherit the land."*

Lesson 8 פ ף ק כ

HaTikva

A12

כֹּל עוֹד בַּלֵּבָב פְּנִימָה נֶפֶשׁ יְהוּדִי הוֹמִיָּה
וּלְפַאֲתֵי מִזְרָח, קָדִימָה, עַיִן לְצִיּוֹן צוֹפִיָּה
עוֹד לֹא אָבְדָה תִּקְוָתֵנוּ, הַתִּקְוָה בַּת שְׁנוֹת אַלְפַּיִם
לִהְיוֹת עַם חָפְשִׁי בְּאַרְצֵנוּ אֶרֶץ צִיּוֹן וִירוּשָׁלַיִם.

kol od ba-le-VAV p-nee-MA, **NE**-fesh y-**HOO**-dee ho-mee-YA
ool-fa-a-TAY meez-RAKH ka-dee-MA, a-YEEN l-tsee-YON tso-fee-YA
od lo av-DA teek-va-**TAY**-noo, ha-teek-VA bat sh-not al-**PAI**-yeem
lee-YOT am khof-SHEE b-ar-**TSAY**-noo, **E**-rets tsee-YON vee-roo-sha-**LAI**-yeem

As long as in the heart, within, a Jewish soul still yearns,
And onward, toward the ends of the east, an eye still gazes toward Zion;
Our hope is not yet lost, the hope of two thousand years,
To be a free people in our land, the land of Zion and Jerusalem.

B - Writing

Script	Practice then make flashcards	Block	Letter	
ߥ		פ	פ	B1
ƒ		ף	ף	B2
ק		ק	ק	B3
כ		כ	כ	B4

In script, the end of **TSA**-dee soFEET goes up and the Pay so-FEET goes down. B5

62

Hebrew with Joy!   Lesson 8   פ ף ק כ

C - Root

Word Meaning	Key Word	Root Meaning	Root	
holy	קָדוֹשׁ	holy, set apart	ק.ד.שׁ	C1

C2   קִדּוּשׁ   Sanctification - Shabbat Blessing over the Wine (in Lesson 5)

C3   רוּחַ הַקוֹדֶשׁ   Read and translate: _____ _____

C4   Write the Hebrew word for "holy" then make a flashcard for the key word *and* the root: ------------------ ------------------

D - Exception Vowel

Example	Sound	Vowel	
כָּל = kol	"o" as in fl<u>ow</u>	ָ	D1

D2   Make a flashcard noting that it is an "exception" vowel:

D3   כָּל   all/everything   (כָּל sounds like "kol")

D4   כָּל הַכָּבוֹד   All the honor/glory! (Well done!)

D5   הַכָּל   "the all" is in order (everything's OK)
     b-**SE**-der

D6   כָּל־הָאָרֶץ   All (of) the earth   (כָּל sounds like "khol")

D7   Read and translate the words you know:

קָדוֹשׁ קָדוֹשׁ קָדוֹשׁ יְהוָה צְבָאוֹת
מְלֹא כָל־הָאָרֶץ כְּבוֹדוֹ:

"Holy, holy, holy, is Adonai - The LORD of hosts!
The whole earth is full of His glory." Isaiah 6:3

Hebrew with Joy! Lesson 8 פ ף ק כ

Group Memory Game – *Cut or photocopy this page, then cut out the pieces. Place the pieces on a table with the words facing down and mix well. Player 1 turns over two cards to see if they match (Hebrew with English meaning.) If they do, player 1 keeps the pair and turns over two more. If they don't match, player 2 takes a turn. Play continues until all pairs are matched. Player with the most pairs wins.*

שְׁמַע	life	תּוֹרָה
blessed	קָדוֹשׁ	love
יְהוָה	instruction	holy
hear	שַׁבָּת	LORD
אַהֲבָה	Sabbath	שָׁלוֹם
חַיִּים	בָּרוּךְ	peace

65

Hebrew with Joy! Lesson 8 פ ף ק כ

_____ שֵׁם   # Exercises Lesson 8

Rearrange the letters and vowels in the following **key** words.
In the chart, write the correct Hebrew words and their English translations:

English translation	Key Hebrew Word		
		בְּאֶחָד	.1
		יִסְמַח	.2
		רְתוֹה	.3
Sabbath	שַׁבָּת	תבָּשׁ	.4
		וּרְךְבָּ	.5
		דקָשׁוֹ	.6
		וּמְשָׁל	.7
		מֹשְׁעַ	.8

.9 Practice reading and writing each combination five times in block or script:

כָּל --

קִי --

פִּי --

עַף --

Write the correct form of Pay in the following words then translate to English:

.10 נֶ[ ]שׁ _____ שׁוֹ[ ]ר _____ אֵ[ ]ל Alef _____

.11 What is the English meaning of כָּל? _____

.12 Write in *Hebrew* the name for the Israeli National Anthem: _____

.13 Write in *English* the name for the Israeli National Anthem: _____

67

Exercises Lesson 8

Kadosh

by Elisheva Shomrom (from Isaiah 6:3)
English words by Paul Wilbur

Listen to a version of "Kadosh" (on YouTube) then fill in the missing Hebrew and English words below: (Notice that each line is repeated twice!)   14.

עִבְרִית

	קָדוֹשׁ		קָדוֹשׁ
		קָדוֹשׁ	
	צְבָאוֹת	אֱלֹהִים	
	צְבָאוֹת		יְהוָה
וְיָבוֹא	וְהֹוֶה	הָיָה	אֲשֶׁר
וְיָבוֹא	וְהֹוֶה		אֲשֶׁר

English

Holy		holy	
	holy		
(O) LORD		(LORD of) Hosts	
	(our) God		
Who		and (who) is	
	was		and (who) is to come

Hebrew with Joy!   Lesson 9   ש ס ט ג

Lesson 9   שׁ ס ט ג

> **Israeli Phrase**
> Happy Holiday!   khag sa-**ME**-akh!

A - Letters

Sound	Name	Letter	
"s" as in <u>s</u>on	Shin (dot on the left)	שׂ	A1
"s" as in <u>s</u>on	**SA**-mekh	ס	A2
"t" as in <u>t</u>op (has a *top* hole)	Tet	ט	A3
"g" as in <u>g</u>ap (has a *gap*)	**GI**-mel	ג	A4

Read the following lines two times:

A5   שֶׁ שַׁ סִי סוּ טוּ טִי עָג אֵיט

A6   שִׂים סוֹט טַי גִין סִי גִין סַג גוּת טָךְ

Read and translate the following two lines:

A7   סֻכּוֹת   פֶּסַח   סֵדֶר   טוֹב   חֶסֶד

A8   _____   _____   order   _____   kindness

A9   טַלִּית   טָהוֹר   עֹנֶג שַׁבָּת   יִשְׂרָאֵל

A10   prayer shawl   clean/pure   _____   _____

A11   *The original meaning of* יִשְׂרָאֵל *"Israel" comes from two roots:* ש.ר.ה *"to persevere, have power, strive or contend" and* א.ל *"God." Only through the power of our Mighty God has Israel persevered for more than two thousand years!*

69

Lesson 9 ג ט ס ש *Hebrew with Joy!*

Read the following Scripture:

לֵב טָהוֹר בְּרָא־לִי אֱלֹהִים   A12

Create in me a clean heart, O God   Psalm 51:12

מוֹעֲדִים

Leviticus 23:2 "Speak to the sons of Israel and tell them, 'These are my appointed times, the festivals of Adonai, which you are to proclaim to be sacred assemblies.'" Scripture is clear about these מוֹעֲדִים "God Appointments" on His holy calendar. They are to be eternal reminders of His faithfulness to us. Translate these and share what they represent:

שָׁבוּעוֹת   שַׁבָּת   סֻכּוֹת   פֶּסַח   A13

B - Vowels

Sound: "ooey" as in gooey	וּי	B1
Sound: "oy" as in toy or "oy" vay! (Yiddish for "Oh my goodness!")	וֹי	B2

Make flashcards for the above vowel combinations: B3

Read and translate:

גּוֹיִים _____   גּוּר _____   רָאוּי _____ worthy   B4

אַתָּה רָאוּי _____   B5

C - Root

Word Meaning	Key Word	Root Meaning	Root	
joy	שִׂמְחָה	joyful	שׂ.מ.ח	C1

Read and translate:

שִׂמְחַת תּוֹרָה _____   C2

שִׂמְחַת תּוֹרָה

is celebrated on the eighth day of סֻכּוֹת (Feast of Tabernacles). During this joyous holiday, the Torah scroll readings are finished for the year and the Torah is rolled back to the beginning (Gen. 1:1) to start a new yearly cycle. The men dance around the Torah and carry it through the neighborhood. It is indeed a joyous celebration of God's Holy Word!   C3

Hebrew with Joy! — Lesson 9 — ג ט ס שׁ

חַג _____ שָׂמֵחַ

When greeting someone during a holiday in Israel, it is customary to add the name of the holiday between "khag" and "sa-ME-akh"
Read and translate the following greetings:

חַג סֻכּוֹת שָׂמֵחַ!
חַג פֶּסַח שָׂמֵחַ!
חַג חֲנֻכָּה שָׂמֵחַ!

C4

D - Writing

Script	Practice then make flashcards	Block	Letter	
e		שׁ	שׁ	D1
ס		ס	ס	D2
ט		ט	ט	D3
ג		ג	ג	D4

Write the Hebrew word for "joy" then make a flashcard for the key word *and* the root.   D5

Hebrew with Joy!   Lesson 9   שׁ ס ט ג

Match the Roots and Key Words! *Make two copies of Game Page 1 and Page 2. Cut out the pieces and give each team a complete set. The teams turn the pieces face down on a table. On a signal from the leader, teams turn over all of the pieces and try to match the root, meaning of the root, key Hebrew word from the root & English meaning of the word. First team to match all 9 sets wins the game.*

Game Page 1

joyful	שַׁבָּת	hit the mark
שׁ.ל.ם	ב.ר.ך	completion, wholeness
life	תּוֹרָה	blessed
שׁ.מ.ע	שְׁמַע	hear & obey
חַיִּים	בָּרוּךְ	rest, stop
א.ה.ב	peace	שִׂמְחָה

Hebrew with Joy!   Lesson 9   ש ט ג

Game Page 2

ח.י.ה	love	live
instruction	אַהֲבָה	holy
שׂ.מ.ח	bless, kneel	י.ר.ה
ק.ד.שׁ	holy	Joy
Sabbath	שׁ.ב.ת	קָדוֹשׁ
hear	שָׁלוֹם	love

Hebrew with Joy!   Lesson 9   שׁ ט ג

Exercises Lesson 9   שֵׁם _____

1. Read and translate these Hebrew words:

בָּרוּךְ   תּוֹרָה   אַהֲבָה   שַׁבָּת   יְהוָה   שָׁלוֹם   רוּחַ

חַיִּים   קָדוֹשׁ   שְׁמַע   שִׂמְחָה   יִשְׂרָאֵל

2. Write the English letter that matches the עִבְרִית:

A. Happy holiday
B. Good morning
C. Sabbath peace
D. Thanks a lot. You're welcome.
E. My name is Dan. Nice to meet you.
F. Holy Spirit
G. All the honor/glory
H. Blessed are you, LORD.
I. Hear, Israel
J. Hello/Goodbye friends

	כָּל הַכָּבוֹד
C	שַׁבָּת שָׁלוֹם
	שְׁמַע יִשְׂרָאֵל
	שְׁמִי דָן. נָעִים מְאֹד.
	בּוֹקֶר טוֹב
	חַג שָׂמֵחַ
	תּוֹדָה רַבָּה. בְּבַקָּשָׁה
	שָׁלוֹם חֲבֵרִים
	בָּרוּךְ אַתָּה יְהוָה
	רוּחַ הַקּוֹדֶשׁ

3. Write the Key Words in Hebrew:

	instruction		life
	love		LORD
שַׁבָּת	Sabbath		blessed
	hear		peace
	joy		holy

4. Write the *root* letters meaning "joy"   _____

5. Write the Hebrew for "Happy holiday!"   _____

6. Complete your flashcard set for all the letters, vowels and key words Practice them every day until you know them by heart!

Exercises Lesson 9

Fill in the missing English translations:

אוֹתְךָ!	אוֹהֵב	אֲנִי	אַבָּא	שָׁלוֹם	Man writing to his Father	7.
you (m)	love (m)	I		Hello		
אוֹתָךְ	אוֹהֶבֶת	אֲנִי	אַבָּא	שָׁלוֹם	Woman writing to her Father	8.
you (m)	love (f)		Daddy			

Practice your עִבְרִית by writing the prayer above in Hebrew:
(If you are a man, write line 7 from above, if you are a woman, write line 8)

9. עִבְרִית _____
   _____

Write your own prayer!

10. Write your own new Hebrew prayer to Adonai! Try to use as many Hebrew words as you can! Refer to the Dictionary in the Appendix to help you:

_____
_____
_____

11. Translate your prayer into English:

_____
_____
_____

Lesson 10
Reading Scriptures

A – Syllable Breaks

To help read Hebrew words, add syllable lines to the Scripture – one sounded vowel per syllable	A1
בָּ|רוּךְ הַ|בָּא בְּ|שֵׁם יְיָ*	A2
*Syllable marks are not used in the unpronounceable name of God	A3

Add syllable lines then read the Scriptures:

זָכוֹר אֶת־יוֹם הַשַּׁבָּת לְקַדְּשׁוֹ   A4

Remember the Sabbath day to keep it holy. (Exodus 20:8)

יֵצֶר סָמוּךְ תִּצֹּר שָׁלוֹם שָׁלוֹם   A5

You keep in perfect peace one whose mind is stayed on You. (Isaiah 26:3)

עֵץ־חַיִּים הִיא לַמַּחֲזִיקִים בָּהּ   A6

She is a tree of life to those who embrace her. (Proverbs 3:18)

לֵב טָהוֹר בְּרָא־לִי אֱלֹהִים   A7

Create in me a clean heart, O God. (Psalm 51:12(10))

גַּל־עֵינַי וְאַבִּיטָה נִפְלָאוֹת מִתּוֹרָתֶךָ׃   A8

Open my eyes, so I may behold wonders from Your Torah. (Psalm 119:18)

Lesson 10
Reading Scriptures

Hebrew with Joy!

B – Cantillation Accent Marks

*The special markings in Biblical Hebrew are called "**Cantillation Marks**." They have three purposes: First, they show the accented syllable of each word. Second, they divide verses into smaller units of meaning and put phrases together. Last, the marks have a musical value allowing the "Cantors" (song leaders) to chant the verses.*	B1

When you are pronouncing a Hebrew word from the Scriptures, there could be many cantillation marks. One of them shows the accented syllable.	B2
גַּל־עֵינַי וְאַבִּיטָה נִפְלָאוֹת מִתּוֹרָתֶךָ:	B3

Read out loud the Scripture below. Use syllable lines and the accent marks to help you pronounce the Hebrew correctly.

B4

עִבְדוּ אֶת־יְהוָה בְּשִׂמְחָה

Serve/work for/worship A<small>DONAI</small> with joy! (Psalm 100:2)

The root for "serve," ע.ב.ד also means "work" and "worship". Everything we do in life, as we work, serve or worship, should always be our very best effort for our wonderful LORD...<u>and</u> it should be done with JOY!	B5

Hebrew with Joy!
Reading Scriptures

Lesson 10

C – Continuing Your Hebrew!

Using your flashcards, continue to practice the letters, vowels, key words and roots you have learned. — C1

As you study the Scriptures, when you come to a verse that stands out, read it out loud in Hebrew. — C2

To welcome in the Shabbat on Friday evening (Erev Shabbat), read the Hebrew prayers on the Shabbat Handout in Chapter 5. — C3

During your quiet times, write a Hebrew prayer to Adonai in your journal. Use the dictionary in this book to help you. — C4

Use a Hebrew Bible or online Hebrew Bible program to find your favorite Scripture. Then read and write it in Hebrew as a blessing to Adonai. — C5

Use the free Hebrew with Joy! Video Lessons to reinforce what you have learned. https://hebrewwithjoy.com/hebrew-with-joy-video-lessons-2/   Password: HWJvideos — C6

Review the Hebrew Resources page and add a new Hebrew or Bible app or program to your phone or computer. — C7

Teach others how to learn Hebrew! This is the best way to reinforce what you have learned. Please share your new knowledge by teaching others who have a heart for God, His Land and His People! The Video lessons (link above) can be helpful for teaching individuals, families, home school, bible study or other groups. — C8

Move on in the *Hebrew with Joy!* series! The second book, **Biblical Hebrew with Joy!** will take you deeper into the Hebrew Scriptures by learning grammar tips and increasing your Biblical vocabulary and roots. The second book also includes a free video series so that you can learn on your own. As always, studying with an accountability person or group will be a tremendous help! — C9

Praise Puzzle: *Each Hebrew combination below sounds like an English word. As you sound each one out, write the English words in the left column, then read the sentences in English.*

My...	מַי בֶּסט פְרֶנד	1
Who is my best friend?	הוא אז מַי בֶּסט פְרֶנד?	2
He helps me to grow.	הֶע הֶלְפְּס מיא תֶע גְרוה.	3
He hears my voice.	הֶע הִירְז מַי בויש.	4
He likes me a lot.	הֶע לַיקְס מיא אֵי לָט.	5
He holds my head up.	הֶע הוֹלְדז מַי הֶד אַפּ.	6
He never leaves me.	הֶע נֶעֶר לִיבְז מיא.	7
He guides my steps.	הֶע גִידז מַי שְׁטֶפְּס.	8
Do you know who my best friend is?	דֶע יוא נוֹה הוא מַי בֶּסט פְרֶנד אז?	9
He is my Lord, God of my heart!	הֶע אז מַי לוֹרְד, גַד אֶב מַי הָרְת!	10

Hebrew with Joy!
Reading Scriptures

Lesson 10

כָּל הַכָּבוֹד!

Well done! You have now learned to read and write עִבְרִית. May Hebrew truly be a JOY as you go deeper in your study of the Hebrew Scriptures with God's Holy Language!

Lesson 10
Reading Scriptures

Hebrew with Joy!

**Please complete this page without looking up any answers.
After checking your answers, compare this quiz to the Pre-Quiz.

Name: _____

Date: _____

Post-Quiz

A. Was this your first Hebrew class? _____

B. Match the letters to their sounds:

ע _3_ 1. d

צ ___ 2. r

פּ ___ 3. silent

ר ___ 4. s

ק ___ 5. k

ד ___ 6. ts

ס ___ 7. p

C. Match the sounds:

תַ ___ 1. too

תוֹ ___ 2. tee

תָ ___ 3. tie

תוּ ___ 4. tah

תִי ___ 5. toe

תֵי ___ 6. teh

תֵ ___ 7. tay

D. Match the words:

שְׁמַע ___ 1. life

קָדוֹשׁ ___ 2. blessed

חַיִּים ___ 3. holy

בָּרוּךְ ___ 4. hear

E. Match the roots:

שׂ.מ.ח ___ 1. hit the mark

י.ר.ה ___ 2. love

שׁ.ב.ת ___ 3. joy

א.ה.ב ___ 4. rest/stop

E. Write in Hebrew: Sabbath Peace _____

86

Hebrew with Joy!
Reading Scriptures

Hebrew With Joy!
Class Evaluation

If you are a part of a class, give or email a copy of this evaluation to your instructor and send a copy to hebrewwithjoy33@gmail.com. Todah rabah! Also, if you are studying on your own, would you be willing to write a book review that would encourage others to buy the book? Please post it through Amazon.com. Todah!

1. How would you rate this class on a scale of 1 to 5 (5 being the highest) _____

2. What did you like most about the class?

3. What suggestion/s do you have that would make the class better?

4. Would you be willing to write a book review that would encourage others to buy the book? Please post it through Amazon.com (search for: Hebrew with Joy Learn Simple Hebrew with the Scriptures)

תּוֹדָה רַבָּה!

Appendix

Lesson Fill-Ins

Fill-Ins from right to left!	Line	Lesson
daughter	B7	1
Sabbath	B11	1
peace/ hello/goodbye	B4	2
LORD, day, instruction	A7	3
name	D5	3
Moses, the name	D8	3
the peace, the Sabbath, the instruction	E2	3
God/god, son, Daddy, amen/so be it	A8	4
see you later, candlestick/lamp, Solomon	C12	4
God, hear/listen	C15	4
Rachel, king	A7	5
Ruth, hallelujah, blessed	D6	5
David, thanks	A8	6
weeks, Hebrew, friends	A11	6
and hear, and Moshe	B2	6
braided bread, spirit/wind/breath	E5	6
appointed times, going up/immigrate to Israel	E7	6
שָׁלוֹם, friends, see you later!	G1	6
tree	A5	7
doorpost/prayer box, Feast of Lots	A9	7
Zion, son of (the) commandment	A11	7
our God	B4	7
Jerusalem, to life, life	B6	7
ram's horn	A8	8
Feast of Dedication, Day of Atonement, the hope	A10	8
Holy Spirit	C3	8
Feast of Tabernacles, Passover, good	A8	9
Sabbath delight, Israel	A10	9
gentile/nation, gentiles/nations	B4	9
You are worthy	B5	9
Joy (of) Torah	C2	9
זָכוֹר אֶת־יוֹם הַשַּׁבָּת לְקַדְּשׁוֹ	A4	10
יֵצֶר סָמוּךְ תִּצֹּר שָׁלוֹם שָׁלוֹם	A5	10
עֵץ־חַיִּים הִיא לַמַּחֲזִיקִים בָּהּ	A6	10
לֵב טָהוֹר בְּרָא־לִי אֱלֹהִים	A7	10
גַּל־עֵינַי וְאַבִּיטָה נִפְלָאוֹת מִתּוֹרָתֶךָ:	A8	10
עִבְדוּ אֶת־יְהוָה בְּשִׂמְחָה	B4	10

Lesson 5
Answers to Self-Quiz
(from top to bottom)
A. 10,13,11,9, 14,8,12,15
B. 5,7,3,1,2,6,4
C. 2,3,5,4,1,6
D. 2,3,2,1,5,4, 5,1,6,4

Lesson 10-Praise Puzzle
1. My Best Friend
2. Who is my best friend?
3. He helps me to grow
4. He hears my voice
5. He likes me a lot
6. He holds my head up
7. He never leaves me
8. He guides my steps
9. Do you know who my best friend is?
10. He is my LORD, God of my heart

Exercise Answers:
Link:
HebrewWithJoy.com/hwj-exercise-answers
PW: answers

Hebrew Letters

Sound	Name	Script	Block	Letter
silent	**A**-lef			א
b as in **b**ar	**Bet** (with a dot)			בּ
v as in **v**ictory	Bet (without a dot)			ב
g as in **g**ap	**GI**-mel			ג
d as in **d**oor	**DA**-let			ד
h as in **h**oly	Hay			ה
v as in **v**ictory	Vav			ו
z as in **z**eal	**ZA**-yin			ז
kh as in Ba**ch**	Khet			ח
t as in **t**op	Tet			ט
y as in **y**es	Yud/Yod			י
k as in **k**ing	Kaf (with a dot)			כּ
kh as in Ba**ch**	Kaf (without a dot)			כ
kh as in Ba**ch**	Kaf so-FEET			ך
l as in **l**ight	**LA**-med			ל
m as in **m**olehill	Mem			מ
m as in **m**olehill	Mem so-FEET			ם
n as in **n**ame	Nun			נ
n as in **n**ame	Nun so-FEET			ן

Hebrew Letters (cont.)

Sound	Name	Script	Block	Letter
s as in son	SA-mekh	ס	ס	ס
silent	AY-in	ע	ע	ע
p as in pray	Pay (with a dot)	פּ	פּ	פּ
f as in faith	Pay (without a dot)	פ	פ	פ
f as in faith	Pay so-FEET	ף	ף	ף
ts as in roots	TSA-dee	צ	צ	צ
ts as in roots	TSA-dee so-FEET	ץ	ץ	ץ
k as in king	Koof	ק	ק	ק
r as in rest	Raysh	ר	ר	ר
sh as in shine	Shin	שׁ	שׁ	שׁ
s as in son	Shin	שׂ	שׂ	שׂ
t as in toe	Tav	ת	ת	ת

Hebrew Vowels

"a" as in <u>a</u>ll	◌ֱ ◌ָ ◌ַ
"o" as in <u>o</u>ver (dot is **o**ver the letter)	וֹ ◌ֹ
"e" as in <u>e</u>gg (2, 3 or 5 **e**ggs in a basket)	◌ֱ ◌ֶ ◌ֵ
"ee" as in f<u>ee</u>t (the vowel is under the f**ee**t of the letter)	יִ ◌ִ
silent or "uh" as in <u>a</u>bove (one dot **a**bove the other)	◌ְ
"oo" as in t<u>oo</u> ("ooh- it hurts)	וּ ◌ֻ
"akh" as in B<u>ach</u> (exception – at the end of a word)	חַ
"ay" as in l<u>ay</u> ("e" + "ee")	יֵ
"ai" as in p<u>ie</u> ("a" + "ee")	יַ
"o" as in fl<u>ow</u> (exception vowel!)	◌ָ
"oy" as in t<u>oy</u>	וֹי
"ooey" as in g<u>ooey</u>	וּי

98

Hebrew Phrases

	Lesson Phrases				Classroom Phrases		
Less #	English	Transliteration	Hebrew		English	Transliteration	Hebrew
1	hello, goodbye, peace	sha-LOM	שָׁלוֹם		class	kee-TA	כִּיתָּה
1	my name is _____	sh-mee _____.	שְׁמִי _____.		correct	na-KHON	נָכוֹן
2	nice to meet you	na-EEM m-OD	נָעִים מְאוֹד		excellent	me-tsoo-YAN	מְצוּיָן
2	see you later	l-heet-ra-OT	לְהִתְרָאוֹת		finished	**ZE**-o	זֶהוּ
3	good morning	**BO**-ker tov	בּוֹקֶר טוֹב		good	tov	טוֹב
3	good evening	**E**-rev tov	עֶרֶב טוֹב		great!/terrific	**YO**-fee	יוֹפִי
3	good night	**LAI**-la tov	לַיְלָה טוֹב		in Hebrew	b-eev-REET	בְּעִבְרִית
3	have a good week	sha-**VOO**-a tov	שָׁבוּעַ טוֹב		no	lo	לֹא
4	how's it going?	ma neesh-MA?	מָה נִשְׁמַה?		quiet!	**SHE**-ket!	שֶׁקֶט!
4	good, thanks	tov, to-DA!	טוֹב, תּוֹדָה.		quiet, please!	**SHE**-ket b-va-ka-SHA!	שֶׁקֶט בְּבַקָּשָׁה!
4	morning light	**BO**-ker or	בּוֹקֶר אוֹר		students	tal-mee-DEEM	תַּלְמִידִים
5	OK, fine	b-**SE**-der	בְּסֵדֶר		teacher (FS)	mo-RA	מוֹרָה
6	hello, friends bye, friends	sha-LOM kha-ve-REEM	שָׁלוֹם חֲבֵרִים		teacher (MS)	mo-RE	מוֹרֶה
7	thanks very much	to-DA ra-BA	תּוֹדָה רַבָּה		very good	tov m-OD	טוֹב מְאוֹד
7	you're welcome (please)	b-va-ka-SHA	בְּבַקָּשָׁה		what's this/that?	ma ze?	מַה זֶה?
8	all the honor/glory (well done)	kol ha-ka-VOD!	כָּל הַכָּבוֹד!		yes	ken	כֵּן
9	happy holiday!	khag sa-**ME**-akh!	חַג שָׂמֵחַ!				

Hebrew Resources

1. **Blue Letter Bible -** www.blueletterbible.org Free app for phone or computer; has user friendly verse look-up with large easy-to-read Hebrew interlinear (includes vowels!)

2. **Bible Hub -** www.biblehub.com Free app for phone or computer; includes an interlinear option where you can see the Hebrew text with vowels, English word-for-word translation and Strong's concordance

3. **iTranslate -** https://www.itranslate.com Free app that translates English to Hebrew –Free App for Iphone or Ipad *includes Hebrew voice translation.*

4. **Google Translate -** https://translate.google.com Free app for phone or computer

5. **Prolog Hebrew-English Dictionary -** http://learnhebrew.prolog.co.il
   Free app for phone or computer - There is a charge for the complete dictionary
   includes vowels, accents and genders

6. **Bible Gateway -** https://www.biblegateway.com/
   Free Bible program for phone or computer; search for specific Scriptures
   Hebrew translations can be seen side-by-side next to the English!
     A Westminster Leningrad Codex (WLC) for the Tanach (Old Testament)
     B HaBrit HaKhadasha/HaDereck (HHH) for the Brit Khadashah (New Testament)

7. **Serve-A-Verse -** http://www.levsoftware.com/SAV/
   Free version - Choose single verses to hear the Hebrew audio. Paid version – more options

8. **YouVersion –** https://www.youversion.com/the-bible-app/
   Free Bible app for cell phone or computer with same Hebrew translations as Bible Gateway

9. **Touch Bible -** https://www.touchbible.com/touch-bible-loaded
   Free app for cell phone –Bible with Strong's Concordance with roots, Hebrew spelling and vowels

10. **Download Hebrew Fonts –** http://www.tyndale.cam.ac.uk/unicode
    To see an on-screen computer keyboard for typing Hebrew letters and vowels

11. **Hebrew KB –** app for phone that lets you see a Hebrew keyboard and type Hebrew letters and vowels

Scriptural and Cultural Treasures Index

Scriptural and Cultural Treasures	Line	Lesson
Alef	A5	4
Aliyah	E8	6
Bar Mitzvah	A12	7
B'resheet In the Beginning	A4	1
Blessed are You Adonai	E10	5
B'reet Mila - Circumcision	C13	4
Cantillation Marks	B1	10
Chanukah Dreidel Letters	A7	2
HaTikva - National Anthem	A11	8
Hay - Holy Spirit	E3	3
Hay - Open door	A4	3
Holiday Greetings	C4	9
Israel	A11	9
Jerusalem	D3	2
Khai - live	B7	7
Khet - Life	A5	5
Mezuzah	B8	7
Midrash	B4	3
Moadeem - Appointed times	A13	9
Paleo - Hebrew	D7	2
Serve - ע.ב.ד.	B5	10
Sh'ma	D3	4
Shabbat	C7	1
Shabbat Guide		5
Shabbat Shalom Paleo Hebrew	D7	2
Shalom Chaverim song	G2	6
Simkhat Torah	C3	9
Tzitzit - Fringes	A10	7
Unpronounceable Name of God	A9	6
Vav hook	B3	6

Hebrew Dictionary

Less #	English	Transliteration	Hebrew	Less #	English	Transliteration	Hebrew
8	all/everything	kol, khol	כָּל, כֹּל	7	fringes	tsee-tseet	צִיצִית
7	almighty (my breast)	sha-DAI	שַׁדַּי	9	gentile, nation	goy	גּוֹי
4	amen - so be it	a-MEN	אָמֵן	9	gentiles, nations	go-YEEM	גּוֹיִם
6	anointed one	ma-SHEE-akh	מָשִׁיחַ	4	God, god	e-lo-HEEM, el	אֱלֹהִים אֵל
6	appointed times	mo-a-DEEM	מוֹעֲדִים	4	God/my Master	a-do-NAI	אֲדוֹנָי
5	blessed	ba-ROOKH	בָּרוּךְ	6	going up-Aliyah	a-lee-YA	עֲלִיָה
5	blessing	bra-KHA	בְּרָכָה	9	good	tov	טוֹב
8	blessing over the wine	kee-DOOSH	קִדּוּשׁ	3	good evening	**E**-rev tov	עֶרֶב טוֹב
9	booths, Feast of Tabernacles	soo-KOT	סֻכּוֹת	3	good morning	**BO**-ker tov	בֹּקֶר טוֹב
6	braided bread	kha-LA	חַלָּה	3	good week	sha-**VOO**-a tov	שָׁבוּעַ טוֹב
5	bread	**LE**-khem	לֶחֶם	5	hallelujah	ha-l-loo-YA	הַלְלוּיָהּ
4	candle stick /lamp	m-no-RA	מְנוֹרָה	9	happy holiday	khag sa-**ME**-akh	חַג שָׂמֵחַ
8	charity	ts-da-KA	צְדָקָה	4	hear/listen	sh-MA	שְׁמַע
4	covenant	b-reet	בְּרִית	6	heart	lev	לֵב
9	clean/pure	ta-HOR	טָהוֹר	6	Hebrew	eev-REET	עִבְרִית
7	commandment	meets-VA	מִצְוָה	8	holy	ka-DOSH	קָדוֹשׁ
8	community/congregation	k-hee-LA	קְהִילָה	8	Holy Spirit	**ROO**-akh ha-**KO**-desh	רוּחַ הַקֹּדֶשׁ
4	Dad/Daddy	**A**-ba	אַבָּא	8	honor/glory	ka-VOD	כָּבוֹד
1	daughter	bat	בַּת	8	Hope, the	ha-teek-VA	הַתִּקְוָה
6	David	da-VEED	דָּוִד	3	instruction	to-RA	תּוֹרָה
3	day	yom	יוֹם	9	Israel	yees-ra-EL	יִשְׂרָאֵל
8	Day of Atonement	yom kee-POOR	יוֹם כִּפּוּר	7	Jerusalem	y-roo-sha-**LAI**-yeem	יְרוּשָׁלַיִם
8	dedication, Feast of Dedication	kha-noo-KA	חֲנֻכָּה	9	joy	seem-KHA	שִׂמְחָה
9	doorpost, prayer box	m-zoo-ZA	מְזוּזָה	9	Joy of the Torah	seem-KHAT to-RA	שִׂמְחַת תּוֹרָה
8	everything's OK	ha-KOL b-**SE**-der	הַכֹּל בְּסֵדֶר	9	kindness	**KHE**-sed	חֶסֶד
8	everything	ha-KOL	הַכֹּל	5	king	**ME**-lekh	מֶלֶךְ
5	faith	e-moo-NA	אֱמוּנָה	5	knee	**BE**-rekh	בֶּרֶךְ
7	family	meesh-pa-KHA	מִשְׁפָּחָה	7	life	khai-EEM	חַיִּים
6	father	av	אָב	4	light	or	אוֹר
6	friends	kha-ve-REEM	חֲבֵרִים	7	live	khai	חַי

105

Hebrew Dictionary (cont.)

Less #	English	Transliteration	Hebrew	Less #	English	Transliteration	Hebrew
3,5,6	LORD	a-do-NAI, ya, ye-ho-VA, ha-SHEM, Yahweh	יְהֹוָה, יָהּ, יהוה, יְיָ	7	son of (the) commandment	bar meets-VA	בַּר מִצְוָה
7	lots, Festival of Lots	poo-REEM	פּוּרִים	7	sons of	b-NAY	בְּנֵי
6	love - noun	a-ha-VA	אַהֲבָה	8	soul	**NE**-fesh	נֶפֶשׁ
9	love - FS verb	o-**HE**-vet	אוֹהֶבֶת	6	spirit, wind, breath	**ROO**-akh	רוּחַ
9	love - MS verb	o-**HEV**	אוֹהֵב	3	sun	**SHE**-mesh	שֶׁמֶשׁ
6	mercy/mercies	ra-kha-MEEM	רַחֲמִים	3	teacher - FS	mo-RA	מוֹרָה
3	Moses	**MO**-she	מֹשֶׁה	3	teacher - MS	mo-RE	מוֹרֶה
3	mountain	har	הַר	6	thanks	to-DA	תּוֹדָה
3	name	shem	שֵׁם	4	the comer, the one who comes	ha-BA	הַבָּא
6	Noah	**NO**-akh	נֹחַ	8	The Hope	ha-teek-VA	הַתִּקְוָה
9	order	**SE**-der	סֵדֶר	3	the Name	ha-SHEM	הַשֵּׁם
7	our God	e-lo-**HAY**-noo	אֱלֹהֵינוּ	2	there	sham	שָׁם
9	Passover	**PE**-sakh	פֶּסַח	7	this/that	ze	זֶה
2	peace, hello, goodbye	sha-LOM	שָׁלוֹם	7	to life	l-khai-YEEM	לְחַיִּים
4	people	am	עַם	7	tree	ets	עֵץ
8	prayer	t-fee-LA	תְּפִלָּה	7	tree of life	ets khai-YEEM	עֵץ חַיִּים
9	prayer shawl	ta-LEET	טַלִּית	6	turn/return	shoov	שׁוּב
5	Rachel	ra-KHEL	רָחֵל	8	wedding canopy	khoo-PA	חֻפָּה
8	ram's horn	sho-FAR	שׁוֹפָר	6	weeks, Feast of Weeks, Pentecost	sha-voo-OT	שָׁבוּעוֹת
5	Ruth	root	רוּת	5	welcome - MS *Blessed is the one who comes*	ba-ROOKH ha-BA	בָּרוּךְ הַבָּא
1	Sabbath	sha-BAT	שַׁבָּת	5	welcome – plural *Blessed are those who come*	broo-KHEEM ha-ba-EEM	בְּרוּכִים הַבָּאִים
9	Sabbath Delight/meal on Sabbath	**O**-neg sha-BAT	עֹנֶג שַׁבָּת	3	what	ma	מַה
5	salvation	y-shoo-A	יְשׁוּעָה	6	work/serve/worship	a-vo-DA	עֲבוֹדָה
8	sanctification	kee-DOOSH	קִדּוּשׁ	9	worthy	ra-**OO**-ee	רָאוּי
4	see you later	l-hee-tra-OT	לְהִתְרָאוֹת	4	you - FS	at	אַתְּ
4	Solomon	shlo-MO	שְׁלֹמֹה	4	you - MS	a-TA	אַתָּה
4	son	ben	בֵּן	6	Zion	tsee-YON	צִיּוֹן

Notes

Notes

Notes

Notes

Made in the USA
Monee, IL
02 August 2021